becoming like Christ

A Discipleship Guide

Matt Hansen

Becoming Like Christ: *A Discipleship Guide*
Copyright © 2010—2013 by Matt Hansen

First Printing, 2010
Second Printing, 2013

Sponsored by MissionEssentials.com
Published by Essentials Publishing, Lee's Summit, MO

No part of this book may be reproduced, stored in a retrieval system, or transmitted in any form or by any means—electronic, mechanical, photocopy, recording or otherwise—without written permission from the author.

Scripture quotations are taken from the *Holy Bible*, New Living Translation, copyright © 1996, 2004, 2007 by Tyndale House Foundation. Used by permission of Tyndale House Publishers, Inc., Carol Stream, Illinois 60188.

Unless otherwise noted, all images were created by the author. Any additional images or content not created by the author are used with permission and are under the copyright ownership of their respective owner.

All rights reserved.
Printed in the United States of America.

ISBN: 978-0-9888376-1-4 (color version)
ISBN: 978-0-9888376-2-1 (black & white version)

Table of Contents

How to use this Discipleship Guide		5
A Message for the Discipleship Leader		7
Lesson 1	The Christian Journey Begins	8
Lesson 2	Internal Discipline: Faith (part 1 of 3) - Judgment	12
Lesson 3	Internal Discipline: Faith (part 2 of 3) - Atonement	16
Lesson 4	Internal Discipline: Faith (part 3 of 3) - Resurrection	20
Lesson 5	Internal Discipline: Moral Excellence	24
Lesson 6	Internal Discipline: Knowledge	28
Lesson 7	Internal Discipline: Self-Control	32
Lesson 8	External Discipline: Patient Endurance	36
Lesson 9	External Discipline: Godliness	40
Lesson 10	External Discipline: Brotherly Affection	44
Lesson 11	External Discipline: Love	48
Lesson 12	Interpreting the Bible	52
Index of Scripture References		57
Index and Glossary by Subject		59
Large Diagrams from Lessons		65

How To Use This Discipleship Guide

What is the purpose of this Discipleship Guide?
To become like Christ. This guide was written to help new and mature Christian believers become like Christ themselves so that they may likewise disciple others to become like Christ.

"So we tell others about Christ, warning everyone and teaching everyone with all the wisdom God has given us. We want to present them to God, perfect in their relationship to Christ." (Colossians 1:28)

To support the central theme of becoming like Christ, the key scripture on which the entire Discipleship Guide is founded is 2 Peter 1:3—11. It describes eight disciplines for every Christian believer to help them "share in His divine nature" (v. 4); as we follow these disciplines diligently (v. 10), He promises that He will empower us (v. 3—4) to ensure we remain "productive and useful" (v. 8) and "never fall away" (v. 10).

What is the format for each discipleship lesson?
The content for each lesson is designed to fill about one hour of discussion. Naturally, more time can be used to expound on the subject, answer questions, or especially to connect with each other on a more personal level.

Each lesson begins with one introductory page followed by three pages of lesson content. The introductory page for each lesson includes:
- A brief summary with key points
- Inspiring hymn lyrics that are relevant to the lesson
- A Bible reading homework for that lesson
- A progress meter illustrating how far along you are in the Discipleship Guide (example shown at right)

What do the symbols mean throughout the guide?

A quoted passage of scripture. All scriptures come from the New Living Translation (NLT). Even though the passages are written in the guide for convenience, you're encouraged to also look them up in your own Bible.

Discussion questions that pertain to the immediate subject. Please take plenty of time to carefully review these and treat them as opportunities to grow and connect with the one being discipled.

Homework to dig deeper. The homework is designed to encourage daily Bible reading. It would be more effective if the person leading the discipleship also does the same homework and then use the questions as opening discussion during the next lesson.

Answers for the fill-in-the-blanks throughout the lesson. The numbers correspond to the numbers by the blanks. Key words were selected for these answers to help reinforce certain concepts and points from the lesson. Please use these as opportunities to expound on the subject matter with the one being discipled.

An excerpt from a Christian hymn that is relevant to the current topic. Hymns reflect the rich Christian heritage of the Church. They generally convey deep theological concepts into simple, yet powerful poetry that have served the Church for hundreds of years.

A Message for the Discipleship Leader

If this is your first time leading discipleship, then congratulations! This can be a rewarding experience. As well, even though you are the one leading the discipleship, you may also find yourself growing in your own Christian walk.

Suggested Schedule for All Discipleship Lessons

Believe it or not, the goal is not to complete this Discipleship Guide. The goal is to build a trusting relationship that will help encourage the one being discipled into a long and deep journey of becoming like Christ. For example, when a father teaches his daughter to ride a bike, he could provide all the necessary instructions about balance, speed and steering. But she will not fully learn and apply it until her father runs alongside, holds and steers the bike steadily, and gives positive encouragement until she can ride independently. Likewise, discipleship means running alongside a younger believer until he or she can confidently continue on the Christian journey themselves.

This Discipleship Guide has twelve lessons with each lesson designed to cover at least one hour of discussion. With twelve lessons, the discipleship plan could simply involve meeting for twelve weeks to discuss each lesson. It is recommended that only one lesson be discussed at a time so that the content won't become overwhelming.

Please don't feel limited to twelve weeks. A good start could be to spend the first few weeks getting to know each other by sharing each other's testimony and experiences. You could also do light homework such as reading a chapter a day from the book of John and discussing later what you've learned.

Suggested Plan for Each Discipleship Lesson

Here are some suggestions of how you may lead each session in order to help build a relationship:
- Begin and end your session in prayer; include any special needs he or she may have.
- Discuss personal events that occurred since your last meeting (e.g., family, friends, work, church, etc.).
- Discuss the Bible reading homework assigned at your last meeting.
- Talk through the lesson together:
    - Fill in the blanks; use these as key opportunities to go into deeper discussion.
    - Look up each passage in the Bible even though most are already written out.
    - Answer the discussion questions; start by sharing your own answers and experiences.
- Plan for the next meeting and Bible reading homework during the week.

What if they ask a question I can't answer?

You're not expected to have all the answers. This guide is designed to equip you in the basic essentials of Christianity. If you don't have an answer, then let it be a challenge for each of you to find the answer and discuss it next time.

How can I teach others to become like Christ when I have difficulty with it myself?

It's always good to challenge your qualifications to disciple others! We need to humbly be aware of our own constant need for Christ in our lives. So, just relax and be open and honest about your own faults. The point is not to appear like a model Christian, but to point others to the perfect model: Christ Himself.

What if we have a hard time staying on track with this Discipleship Guide?

Don't let following this guide get in the way of building a relationship. Let this guide serve as a guideline rather than a rigorous curriculum with a strict deadline. Get to know each other on a personal level first, then use this guide to support your discussion.

Lesson 1: The Christian Journey Begins

Lesson Summary
- A Christian is someone who has a relationship with God by being adopted into His family. This adoption is only possible because Jesus purchased us to be His very own by taking the punishment we deserve.
- Salvation is like a marriage. It starts with a commitment and continues as a life-long process.
- God's purpose for Christians is to become like Jesus Christ; 2 Peter 1:3—11 states that He will empower us to become like Christ when we diligently follow eight disciplines (explained more in this guide).

Bible Reading: *Galatians*
- Minimum Homework: Read the entire book once (1 chapter per day)
- Stretch Goal: Read the entire book twice (2 chapters per day)

Hymn: My God, Accept My Heart This Day
(written by Matthew Bridges, 1848)

My God, accept my heart this day, and make it always Thine,
That I from Thee no more may stray, no more from Thee decline.
Before the cross of Him who died, behold, I prostrate fall;
Let every sin be crucified, let Christ be all in all.

Anoint me with Thy heavenly grace, adopt me for Thine own,
That I may see Thy glorious face, and worship at Thy throne.
Let every thought, and work, and word, to Thee be ever given;
Then life shall be Thy service, Lord, and death the gate of Heaven.

Lesson 1: The Christian Journey Begins

What does it mean to be a "Christian"?
A Christian isn't just someone who is a follower of Jesus Christ. It isn't just someone who follows His teachings or has a high respect for Him. Following Jesus as a Christian is like a young boy following after his father – he wants to look like him, talk like him, do what he does, and grow up to be just like him.

Becoming like Christ is more than just asking "_____"[1]; Christian acts don't make us Christian. Just as a boy following his father's actions are only meaningful because of their father-son relationship, in the same way our actions are only meaningful when we first have a _____[2] with Christ by being adopted into God's family.

How would you have defined what a Christian is before reading this? How does this change your view?

How are we adopted into God's family?
We can only come to God through Jesus Christ who said:

"I am the way, the truth, and the life. No one can come to the Father except through Me." (John 14:6)

It's only through Jesus that we can be adopted into God's family:

"For all who are led by the Spirit of God are children of God...you received God's Spirit when He adopted you as His own children. Now we call Him, 'Abba, Father'. For His Spirit joins with our spirit to affirm that we are God's children." (Romans 8:14-16)

This adoption process occurs when we get "saved" or "born again". Just as an orphan is rescued or saved from his present circumstance of having no mother or father and is adopted into a new family, Christians are rescued or saved from their circumstance of having no _____[3] with God and then being _____[4] into His family.

The adoption process of salvation for Christians can most simply be described as follows:

- God will judge us for our sins and we cannot save ourselves from this "death sentence".
- Although He was innocent, Jesus willingly suffered the death sentence we deserve.
- God will _____[5] Jesus' death for ours to set us free from our death sentence.

Would you consider yourself to be a part of God's family? Why or why not?

What do I do now that I'm saved and part of God's family?
The process of salvation is only the beginning. It's like the wedding day for newlyweds – it's a wonderful time of joy and celebration, but it's only the beginning of a journey they promise to share until death. For Christians, the "wedding day" is called _____[6] – the moment our Christian journey begins. But what happens after that?

Lesson 1: The Christian Journey Begins (continued)

The salvation process through the life of a Christian can be summarized by the following four steps:

Salvation begins and continues →

2. Justification (born again)   **4. Glorification** (Death)

Our lives over time

1. Condemnation   **3. Sanctification**

1 God's "death sentence" _____ [7] we were adopted into His family.
- We **need** to be saved
- Enslaved by **practice** of sin

2 When we _____ [8] to trust in Christ and were adopted into His family.
- When we **were** saved
- Free from **penalty** of sin

3 When we _____ [9] to become like Christ since we're part of God's family.
- We are **being** saved
- Free from **power** of sin

4 Our _____ [10] inheritance because we're part of God's family.
- When we **will be** saved
- Free from **presence** of sin

See page 65 for a larger view of this diagram

If you consider yourself to be a Christian (a part of God's family and trusting in Him for salvation), then you are now living in the _____ [11] process where you are becoming like Christ.

How do I become like Christ?

If Jesus is perfect and never sinned, then how can God ever expect us to be like Him? The answer is that we can't – not in our own strength, that is. We can never become like Christ until we first understand that it's impossible for us to be like Him by our own effort. Even so, the wonderful part of this sanctification process is that Jesus gives us the _____ [12] to become like Him.

> *"By His divine power, God has given us everything we need for living a godly life...He has given us great and precious promises...that enable you to share His divine nature..." (2 Peter 1:3-4)*

> *"For God is working in you, giving you the desire and the power to do what pleases Him." (Philippians 2:13)*

So our Christian journey _____ [13] with faith in Christ where we are _____ [14] by Christ to reach a _____ [15] of becoming like Christ. It begins, ends, is always about, and is always for Christ!

What does God promise if I try to become like Christ?

Read 2 Peter 1:3-11. It is a passage that explains how to become like Christ. It also describes that if we are faithful in our pursuit to become like Christ, then God promises the following:

- We will "escape the world's _____ [16] caused by human desires" (v 4)
- We will "be more _____ [17]...in [our] knowledge of our Lord Jesus Christ" (v 8)
- We will never be "short-sighted or blind, forgetting [we] have been cleansed from [our] old sins" (v 9)
- We will "never _____ [18] away" (v 10)
- We will be given "a grand entrance into the eternal Kingdom of our Lord and Savior Jesus Christ" (v 11)

> *Are these promises encouraging for your Christian walk? How have you struggled with these in the past?*

Lesson 1: The Christian Journey Begins (continued)

These promises sound great! So what do I do now?
Peter states that we should "make every effort to respond to God's promises" (v 5). He describes these as eight disciplines, four that are internal disciplines and four that are external disciplines:

External Disciplines:
These are visible by others and should be solidly based on the internal disciplines

Internal Disciplines:
These are generally not visible by others and are like layers of underground bedrock on which the external disciplines are built

See page 66 for a larger view of this diagram

How can I learn more about these disciplines?
This discipleship study will explain these disciplines in greater detail in order to help us become more like Christ. It will begin with faith (the first discipline) by describing the _____[19] of the gospel (judgment, Christ's atonement and resurrection), and the _____[20] and historically traditional views of the Christian beliefs and actions for the remaining disciplines by asking:

- What should *Christians* believe and do about each discipline?
- What did *Jesus* believe and do about each discipline?
- What did *other Christians in Church History* believe and do about each discipline?

 Which of the above disciplines do you feel you do well? Which ones do you need to strengthen?

 Read the book of Galatians this week – one chapter per day (or as a stretch goal read it two times). What parts stood out to you the most? What unique characteristics about Christ does Paul describe? In what ways does this book help you to become more like Christ?

 [1]"What would Jesus do?" (WWJD); [2]relationship; [3]relationship; [4]adopted; [5]substitute; [6]Justification; [7]before; [8]began; [9]grow; [10]future; [11]sanctification; [12]power and ability; [13]begins; [14]empowered; [15]goal; [16]corruption; [17]productive and useful; [18]fall; [19]essentials; [20]biblical

Lesson 2: Faith (part 1) - Judgment

Lesson Summary
- Faith is always demonstrated by our actions. If we have no actions, then our faith is meaningless.
- God reveals Himself to everyone through His creation and His commandments He's written on each person's conscience, which confirms that we have all sinned, are guilty before God and are without excuse.
- Just as a judge cannot set a murderer free no matter how many other good things he's done, God cannot let our sins go unpunished. We are already condemned and deserve His death penalty for our sins.

 **Bible Reading:** *Colossians*
- Minimum Homework: Read the entire book twice (1 chapter per day)
- Stretch Goal: Read the entire book four times (2 chapters per day)

 Hymn: Salvation Unto Us Has Come
(written by Paul Speratus, 1523)

What God did in His law demand, And none to Him could render
Caused wrath and woe on every hand, For man, the vile offender.
Our flesh has not those pure desires, The spirit of the Law requires, And lost is our condition.

It was a false, misleading dream, That God His Law had given
So sinners could themselves redeem, And by their works gain Heaven.
The Law is but a mirror bright, To bring the inbred sin to light, That lurks within our nature.

The Law reveals the guilt of sin, And makes men conscience-stricken;
The Gospel then doth enter in, The sinful soul to quicken.
Come to the cross, trust Christ, & live; the Law no peace can ever give, no comfort & no blessing.

Faith clings to Jesus' cross alone, And rests in Him unceasing;
And by its fruits true faith is known, With love and hope increasing.
Yet faith alone doth justify, Works serve thy neighbor and supply, The proof that faith is living.

Lesson 2: Faith (part 1 of 3) - Judgment

What is Faith?

Faith is not just what you believe. In the Bible, it's always demonstrated with action (or "works"). Hebrews 11 states what many Christians describe as the "Hall of Faith":

 *"Faith is the confidence that what we hope for will actually happen; it gives us assurance about things we cannot see." (Hebrews 11:1)*

Faith is described here as "confidence" and "assurance". But the rest of Hebrews 11 describes the "Heroes of Faith" not just by what they said they believed, but by their _____ [1] that proved what they believed. Here are examples of some of those heroes:

Hero of Faith	How did they prove their faith?
_____ [2] (v 4)	Brought an acceptable offering
_____ [3] (v 7)	Built a boat
_____ [4] (v 8 & 17)	Left home and sacrificed Isaac
_____ [5] (v 28)	Kept the Passover
_____ [6] (v 30)	Marched around Jericho

We know that these people had faith because their actions demonstrated their beliefs. Just as no one would normally attempt to skydive if they didn't first believe that the parachute would save their life, in the same way we only take action on what we _____ [7].

 "What good is it...if you say you have faith but don't show it by your actions? Don't you remember that...Abraham was shown to be right with God by his actions when he offered his son Isaac on the altar? You see, his faith and his actions worked together. His actions made his faith complete. ...we are shown to be right with God by what we do, not by faith alone." (James 2:14, 21-22, 24)

Beliefs = Actions

As an example, a train consists of both a locomotive and the railcars it pulls. The railcars without the locomotive go nowhere, and the locomotive without the railcars has no purpose.

In the same way, our beliefs and actions are inseparable, but our beliefs always _____ [8] (or give direction to) our actions (just like a locomotive). So it all starts with what we believe.

 If your friends and family were to only look at your actions, what would they think you believe? What actions should you change to be consistent with your beliefs?

Lesson 2: Faith (part 1 of 3) - Judgment (continued)

If it starts with faith, then what should I believe?

As we learned in Lesson 1, the first step a Christian faces is realizing we are under condemnation—the death sentence for those outside of God's family. Then this is followed by justification—the moment when we are _____ [9] into God's family. So how do we go from step 1 to step 2, that is, from condemnation to justification? It begins with God revealing Himself to us.

How does God reveal Himself to us?

Read Psalm 19. As you do, you'll see the three different ways God reveals Himself as outlined below:

Revelation Type	How is God revealed?	To whom is God revealed?	Scripture Ref.
1. General	God's Creation	All People	Psalm 19:1-4 Romans 1:20
2. Special	Our Conscience	All People	Romans 2:14-15
2. Special	God's Commands	Jews first, then other Believers	Psalm 19:7-9 Romans 2:17-20
3. Personal	Our Conviction	Christian Believers	Psalm 19:11-13 Romans 3:19-20
3. Personal	God's Calling	Christian Believers	Psalm 19:14 Romans 3:21-22

God reveals Himself to every human being at a minimum through His _____ [10] and by His commands He engraved in each person's _____ [11]. These all reveal to us that we have "no excuse" (Romans 1:20), "are under the power of sin" (Romans 3:9), and are all "guilty before God" (Romans 3:19). It is only when we humbly recognize this that God can reveal Himself to us personally first by _____ [12] of our sin, then by our responding in faith to His calling.

How has God revealed Himself to you through His commands (the Bible)? How did you respond?

I'm basically a good person, so why do I need conviction?

Actually, the Bible states that no one is "good" according to God's standards. Just as you use a mirror every day to see how you really look, God gave us the _____ [13] like a mirror to let us see how sinful we really look to Him. Why would God want to do that?

Our sin is rebellion to God. It's like we're saying "God, I don't care what you say, I'm going to do things MY way!" By doing that, we're breaking any relationship we could have with Him. When we're not in God's family, we no longer inherit _____ [14].

But God loves us so much that He gave us the ten commandments so that we can see how rebellious and sinful we really are. He did this in order to convict us so that we'd repent and turn back to Him.

Lesson 2: Faith (part 1 of 3) - Judgment (continued)

But my sins aren't that bad, are they?

Sometimes we may think that little white lies aren't as bad as big, serious lies. But God doesn't look at the size of our sins. In fact, Jesus described in Matthew 5—7 (His sermon on the mount) how God considers it sin even when you only commit it in your heart—even if you didn't actually act it out!

"You have heard...'You must not murder'...But I say to you, if you are even angry with someone, you are subject to judgment! ...You have heard the commandment that says, 'You must not commit adultery.' But I say, anyone who even looks at a woman with lust has already committed adultery with her in his heart." (Matthew 5:21-22, 27-28)

Therefore, Jesus raised God's standard that clearly makes everyone _____ [15] of sin. But even if we commit just one sin, the Bible states that we are guilty of breaking ALL of God's laws.

"For the person who keeps all of the laws except one is as guilty as a person who has broken all of God's laws." (James 2:10)

Just like someone who breaks the law and has a warrant for their arrest, when we disobey God and are guilty of breaking His laws, it's like we have a warrant for our arrest until we face Him on Judgment Day.

"anyone who does not believe in Him has already been judged. ...Anyone who doesn't obey the Son will never experience eternal life but remains under God's angry judgment." (John 3:18,36)

But if God is so good, then won't He just forgive us at Judgment?

It's actually *because* He is good that He will NOT simply forgive us. For example, suppose a murderer got caught and while standing before the judge says, "I know I committed this one act of murder, but otherwise I've been good my entire life. I know you're a good judge, so will you forgive me and let me go free?" Should the judge let him go? Of course not! It's because he's a good judge, that He would not let him go free.

In the same way, God cannot let our sin go _____ [16]. We deserve the death sentence (or condemnation) for our sins. We deserve to go to Hell. However, because of God's great love for us, He took upon Himself that death sentence we deserve so that He could "legally" declare that our sin debt was paid in full. We'll learn about that more in the next lesson as we study the atonement through Jesus Christ.

How does this discussion about being guilty and deserving God's death sentence make you feel? Does it concern you? How does this change your view of God?

Read the book of Colossians two times in the week – one chapter per day (or as a stretch goal read it four times). What parts stood out to you the most? What unique characteristics about Christ does Paul describe? In what ways does this book help you to become more like Christ?

[1] actions; [2] Abel; [3] Noah; [4] Abraham; [5] Moses; [6] People of Israel; [7] believe; [8] lead; [9] adopted; [10] creation; [11] conscience; [12] conviction; [13] Ten Commandments; [14] eternal life; [15] guilty; [16] unpunished

Lesson 3: Faith (part 2) - Atonement

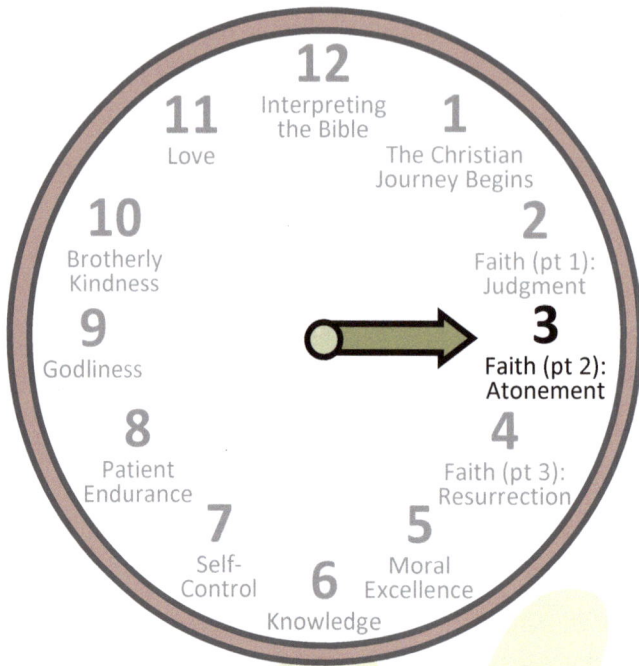

Lesson Summary

- Our sin had broken our relationship with God. Atonement is the process of restoring that relationship.
- To pay our debt of sin to God, we need Jesus Who was both ABLE to save us (He was qualified because he became a human and was sinless) and WILLING to save us (by voluntarily going to the cross).
- To receive this restoration (i.e., to apply Christ's atonement to us), it requires our repentance (turning away from a lifestyle of sin) and dependence (or trust) in Christ alone for our salvation.

Bible Reading: *Philippians*
- Minimum Homework: Read the entire book twice (1 chapter per day)
- Stretch Goal: Read the entire book four times (2 chapters per day)

Hymn: All Ye That Pass By
(written by Charles Wesley, 1779)

For what you have done His blood must atone: The Father hath punished for you His dear Son.
The Lord, in the day of His anger, did lay your sins on the Lamb, and He bore them away.

He dies to atone for sins not His own; Your debt He hath paid and your work He hath done.
Ye all may receive the peace He did leave, Who made intercession, "My Father, forgive!"

For you and for me He prayed on the tree: The prayer is accepted, the sinner is free.
That sinner am I, who on Jesus rely, and come for the pardon God cannot deny.

My pardon I claim; for a sinner I am, a sinner believing in Jesus' name.
He purchased the grace which now I embrace: O Father, Thou know'st He hath died in my place.

His death is my plea; my Advocate see and hear the blood speak that hath answered for me.
My ransom He was when He bled on the cross; and losing His life He hath carried my cause.

Lesson 3: Faith (part 2 of 3) - Atonement

What is Atonement?

It's simply restoring something that's broken, such as repaying a debt, making a restitution for something wrong, or making amends. We learned in Lesson 2 how from a Christian perspective, we are the ones that are in debt to God because of our sin. The debt we owe is a death sentence. Overall, our relationship with God was _____[1].

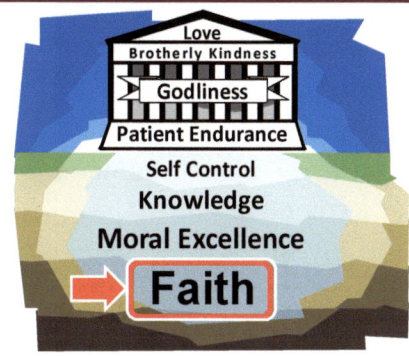

How do we restore our relationship with God?

How do we make amends with Him? How do we make restitution to God for our sins? Quite simply, we never can and we never will! Not without Christ, that is.

Think of it this way. Imagine you were broke and had to pay a fine of $100,000 or else you'd have to go to jail. To avoid going to jail you would need someone who was able and willing:

- ABLE = the person must have $100,000 available
- WILLING = the person must agree to pay the $100,000 fine for you

The richest man in the world may be able to pay your fine because $100,000 may be easy for him to pay. But would he be willing to pay it on your behalf? Probably not.

But our situation is far worse than that! Our debt to God is like being a prison inmate on death row. To pay this debt, it would require someone who was _____[2] and _____[3] to pay our death sentence for us. Our problem is that no one is able to pay our death sentence because everyone is under the same death sentence!

 *"all people...are under the power of sin. As the Scriptures say, 'No one is righteous—not even one.' ...the entire world is guilty before God. ...For everyone has sinned; we all fall short of God's glorious standard." (Romans 3:9-10, 19, 23)*

It's like everyone in the world is stuck on God's death row with us. So it doesn't matter if anyone was willing to pay our death sentence for us, no one is able to pay it anyway.

 Have you ever been in a situation where it seemed impossible to get out? How does that compare to the situation of everyone being stuck on God's death row?

If everyone is guilty, then how can we ever get off of death row?

Jesus was the only One both ABLE and WILLING to pay our death sentence and save us from God's death row. How did He prove He was able and willing?

1. ABLE: Jesus proved He was able by first becoming a _____[4]. This qualifies Him as an acceptable substitute for us on God's death row.

    *"Because [we] are human beings—made of flesh and blood—the Son also became flesh and blood. For only as a human being could He die, and only by dying could He break...the power of death." (Hebrews 2:14)*

Lesson 3: Faith (part 2 of 3) - Atonement (continued)

 *"For it is not possible for the blood of bulls and goats to take away sins. That is why, when Christ came into the world, He said to God, 'You did not want animal sacrifices or sin offerings. But You have given Me a body to offer.'"* (Hebrews 10:4-5)

However, being a human wasn't enough, or else any other human being would qualify. Jesus also had to be completely _____[5] so that He would not be guilty of the same death penalty we are.

"This High Priest of ours [Jesus] understands our weaknesses, for He faced all of the same testings we do, yet He did not sin." (Hebrews 4:15)

"For God made Christ, who never sinned, to be the offering for our sin, so that we could be made right with God through Christ." (2 Corinthians 5:21)

2. WILLING: Jesus proved He was willing by voluntarily suffering the _____[6] we deserve.

"The Father loves Me because I sacrifice My life so I may take it back again. No one can take My life from Me. I sacrifice it voluntarily. For I have the authority to lay it down when I want to and also to take it up again." (John 10:17-18)

"He was oppressed and treated harshly, yet He never said a word. He was led like a lamb to the slaughter. As a sheep is silent before the shearers, He did not open His mouth" (Isaiah 53:7)

Jesus never fought back because He knew the death penalty He suffered is what God would use to substitute for our death penalty. He did that while we were still in sinful _____[7] knowing that one day God will offer us freedom from spiritual death row because Jesus paid our debt in full.

"When we were utterly helpless, Christ came at just the right time and died for us sinners. Now, most people would not be willing to die for an upright person...But God showed His great love for us by sending Christ to die for us while we were still sinners." (Romans 5:6-8)

This _____[8] is the key part of atonement. It is God saving our broken lives from death row, and then restoring us into right-standing with Him. But this atonement doesn't apply to everyone.

> *Think of a time when you did something wrong, but received forgiveness that you didn't deserve. How does that moment compare to knowing God set us free from our death penalty?*

Why doesn't God automatically apply the atonement so everyone can be saved?

God makes His atonement _____[9] to everyone, but as hard as it is to believe, not everyone wants it. It's like someone being freely offered $1,000,000 but refusing to take it. It's as if they either deny their need for the money or they deny the truth of the free offer and then refuse to accept it.

Remember, our sin is a rebellion to God; all of us have completely rejected Him.

 *"All of us, like sheep, have strayed away. We have left God's paths to follow our own. Yet the Lord laid on Him the sins of us all."* (Isaiah 53:6)

 *"But God shows His anger from heaven against all sinful, wicked people who suppress the truth by their wickedness. They know the truth about God because He has made it obvious to them. ...So God abandoned them to do whatever shameful things their hearts desired...They know*

Lesson 3: Faith (part 2 of 3) - Atonement (continued)

God's justice requires that those who do these things deserve to die, yet they do them anyway. Worse yet, they encourage others to do them, too." (Romans 1:18-19, 24, 32)

As we learned in lesson 2, God reveals Himself to every person in a general way (through _____ [10]) and a special way (through our conscience or His _____ [11]). But our sin has hardened our hearts to varying degrees. Someone with a slightly hardened heart may respond more quickly to God than someone with a very hardened heart. Either way, God will hold each person accountable.

But no matter how hard any person's heart is, everyone will eventually be broken.

> *"Anyone who stumbles over that stone [Jesus] will be broken to pieces, and it will crush anyone it falls on." (Matthew 21:44)*

God gives us the opportunity while we're alive to humbly fall on Christ to be broken, or else He will fall on us and crush us at judgment. In either case we will be _____ [12] and confess Jesus as Lord.

> *"that at the name of Jesus every knee should bow, in heaven and on earth and under the earth, and every tongue confess that Jesus Christ is Lord..." (Philippians 2:10-11)*

How do I become broken and receive God's restoration?

God requires two things: 1) REPENTANCE from sin, and 2) DEPENDENCE (or trust) on Christ alone. Both of these require a change in _____ [13] and _____ [14] (as we learned in lesson 2).

Repentance from sin begins with confessing (admitting) our sins to Jesus. It continues with changing our lifestyle by not continuing in the very sin we just confessed. For example, suppose you wanted to go West on a highway but realized you were traveling East. You would need to stop driving East, turn around at the next exit and begin traveling West as originally intended. Likewise, repenting is when you realize you're going the wrong way (in sin), stop yourself from going that wrong direction (stop sinful behavior), and turn around (away from sin) in the direction God intends.

Dependence (or trust) on Christ alone begins with believing in Jesus and the gift of salvation He extends to us through His _____ [15] (taking our death penalty). It continues with confessing (admitting) our need for Jesus and inviting Him to be the Lord of our lives. Just like a skydiver clings to and trusts in his parachute to save his life, we need to cling to and trust in Christ alone for salvation.

> *Would your friends and family think your actions demonstrate repentance from sin and dependence on Christ? How could you demonstrate them even more in your life?*

> Read the book of Philippians two times in the week – one chapter per day (or as a stretch goal read it four times). What parts stood out to you the most? What unique characteristics about Christ does Paul describe? In what ways does this book help you to become more like Christ?

[1] broken; [2] able; [3] willing; [4] human being; [5] sinless; [6] death penalty; [7] rebellion; [8] substitution; [9] available; [10] creation; [11] Word or commands; [12] broken; [13] beliefs; [14] actions; [15] atonement

Lesson 4: Faith (part 3) - Resurrection

Lesson Summary
- As a Christian believer, we are God's children, are at peace with Him and are free from the power of sin; we know this because He places His Spirit in us as a sign and seal of being adopted into His family.
- The Spirit of God raised Jesus from the dead. He placed that same Spirit in us when we got saved so we can have a strong hope and confidence that He will also raise us up to new life.
- Just as a pregnant woman changes her behavior to support the new life inside her, as Christians we need to change our behavior to support the new life (i.e., the Holy Spirit) God placed inside us.

Bible Reading: *Romans*
- Minimum Homework: Read the entire book once (2 chapters per day)
- Stretch Goal: Read the entire book twice (4 chapters per day)

Hymn: One Day
(written by J. Wilbur Chapman, 1908)

One day they led Him up Calvary's mountain, One day they nailed Him to die on the tree;
Suffering anguish, despised and rejected: Bearing our sins, my Redeemer is He!

One day the grave could conceal Him no longer, One day the stone rolled away from the door;
Then He arose, over death He had conquered; Now is ascended, my Lord evermore!

Living, He loved me; dying, He saved me; Buried, He carried my sins far away;
Rising, He justified freely forever; One day He's coming—O glorious day!

Hymn: Crown Him With Many Crowns
(written by Matthew Bridges, 1852)

Crown Him the Lord of life, who triumphed over the grave,
And rose victorious in the strife for those He came to save.
His glories now we sing, who died, and rose on high,
Who died eternal life to bring, and lives that death may die.

Lesson 4: Faith (part 3 of 3) - Resurrection

What is resurrection?

This question isn't so easy to answer because it could mean several things. Most simply, it's when a dead person is revived to life. We've seen this when Jesus raised to life both the widow's son (Luke 7:11-16) and Lazarus (John 11:1-45). Most notably, Jesus was resurrected on the third day after He was crucified. It also refers to a _____[1] when all Christians will be resurrected to new life.

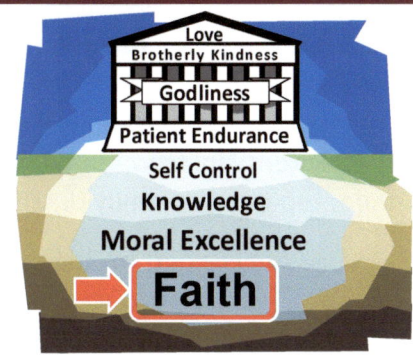

What is the big deal about resurrection?

Why is Jesus' resurrection any better than Lazarus' resurrection? If our atonement was complete because Jesus' death took our _____[2] we deserved (lesson 3), then why is His resurrection so important? He said "It is finished" on the cross; isn't that enough?

Paul tells us that resurrection is a very big deal:

> "And if there is no resurrection of the dead, then Christ has not been raised. And if Christ has not been raised, then your faith is useless and you are still guilty of your sins." (1 Corinthians 15:16-17)

Paul clearly states that Jesus' resurrection is relevant to us and our salvation. So something is unique about Jesus' resurrection (as opposed to the widow's son and Lazarus) and how it applies to our faith. To understand that, we must first understand who we are as Christians.

Who are we as Christians?

In Romans 8, Paul masterfully explains who we are as Christians by comparing us to who we were before we became a Christian. Paul explains that people are either on the side of Death or Life. _____[3] is what separates the two sides (lesson 2) and _____[4] is the only way we can cross from Death to Life (lesson 3). Below is Paul's comparison from Romans 8:

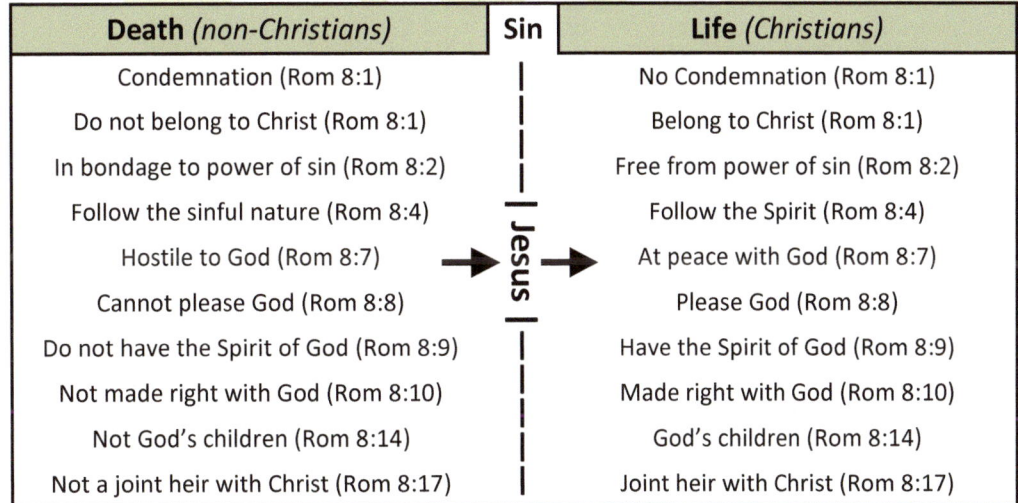

Death (non-Christians)	Sin	Life (Christians)
Condemnation (Rom 8:1)		No Condemnation (Rom 8:1)
Do not belong to Christ (Rom 8:1)		Belong to Christ (Rom 8:1)
In bondage to power of sin (Rom 8:2)		Free from power of sin (Rom 8:2)
Follow the sinful nature (Rom 8:4)		Follow the Spirit (Rom 8:4)
Hostile to God (Rom 8:7)	Jesus	At peace with God (Rom 8:7)
Cannot please God (Rom 8:8)		Please God (Rom 8:8)
Do not have the Spirit of God (Rom 8:9)		Have the Spirit of God (Rom 8:9)
Not made right with God (Rom 8:10)		Made right with God (Rom 8:10)
Not God's children (Rom 8:14)		God's children (Rom 8:14)
Not a joint heir with Christ (Rom 8:17)		Joint heir with Christ (Rom 8:17)

The "Life" characteristics above describe how God sees Christians. Remember, a Christian is someone who has a relationship with God by being _____[5] into His family ; we were adopted into His family not by anything we have done, but only through Jesus Christ (lesson 1).

Lesson 4: Faith (part 3 of 3) - Resurrection (continued)

Christianity is a family, not a club

As Christians, it's easy to think of our relationship to God like a club membership requiring annual dues or else our membership will expire. But that way of thinking implies that our membership is based on our actions. Instead, God describes it as a permanent family relationship that began when we were adopted into His family (Justification) upon demonstrating true faith in Him (lesson 2).

A Christian is a part of God's family, has His Spirit, belongs to Him, pleases Him, and is at peace with Him. As such, we are no longer slaves to our _____^{6}; we neither need to listen nor obey it (Rom 8:12). Romans 8 is like God's official adoption papers that certify we are now in His family.

When have you had strong confidence in something and it influenced your behavior positively? How would your behavior change if you could be more confident in your relationship with God?

How can we be confident that we're a part of God's family?

When you first became a Christian, God deposited His Holy Spirit in you as a guarantee of your adoption:

"...when you believed in Christ, He identified you as His own by giving you the Holy Spirit... The Spirit is God's guarantee that He will give us the inheritance He promised and that He has purchased us to be His own people." (Ephesians 1:13-14)

Being a part of God's family was His plan from the beginning—His plan to have us become like Christ:

"For God knew His people in advance, and He chose them to become like His Son, so that His Son would be the firstborn among many brothers and sisters. And having chosen them, He called them to come to Him. And having called them, He gave them right standing with Himself. And having given them right standing, He gave them His glory." (Romans 8:29-30)

By giving us right standing with God because of Jesus, we can boldly approach Him with confidence:

"...we can boldly enter heaven's Most Holy Place because of the blood of Jesus. By His death, Jesus opened a new and life-giving way ...let us go right into the presence of God with sincere hearts fully trusting Him. For our guilty consciences have been sprinkled with Christ's blood to make us clean... Let us hold tightly without wavering to the hope we affirm, for God can be trusted to keep His promise." (Hebrews 10:19-23)

But our hope isn't just based on God's promise; He also confirmed it by swearing an oath:

"God also bound Himself with an oath, so that those who received the promise could be perfectly sure that he would never change His mind. So God has given both His promise and His oath. These two things are unchangeable because it is impossible for God to lie. Therefore, we who have fled to Him for refuge can have great confidence as we hold to the hope that lies before us. This hope is a strong and trustworthy anchor for our souls." (Hebrews 6:17-19)

Bottom line: The same Spirit of God that raised Jesus from the dead was deposited into us as a guarantee for our own resurrection and inheritance in Christ. God went above and beyond by making both a _____^{7} and an _____^{8} so we can be 100% confident that He will fulfill it. If God never raised Jesus from the dead, then He would've broken His promise and oath and we would also have no hope.

Lesson 4: Faith (part 3 of 3) - Resurrection (continued)

How does Jesus' death, burial and resurrection affect our salvation?

The Bible describes our salvation like a legal transaction where God wipes away our debt and makes a "promissory note" (like a promise to pay) for our future _____ [9]. Below is an illustration:

1. Before Salvation (Indebted by Sin)		2. After Salvation (Work of Atonement)		3. After Salvation (Work of Resurrection)	
What we have	What we owe	What we have	What we owe	What we have	What we owe
$0	$1,000,000	$0	$0	$1,000,000	$0

God's Mercy Erases Debt — God's Grace Makes Deposit

See page 67 for a larger view of this diagram

Comparing Assurance of Salvation with Pregnancy

A woman's pregnancy can be closely compared to a new Christian in 3 different ways:

	A Pregnant Woman *(Baby Inside)*	**A Christian** *(God's Spirit inside)*
1. Personal Assurance	Slight at first, but grows in time (e.g., pregnancy test, ultrasound, belly growing, etc.)	Slight at first, but grows in time (e.g., warm feeling, peace, weight lifted, etc.)
2. Assurance from Others	Based solely on woman's word, but grows when they see outward proof (e.g., woman's belly growing)	Based solely on Christian's word, but grows when they see outward proof (e.g., fruit, faith in action)
3. Change in Behavior	As her assurance in pregnancy grows, she is more supportive of the new life inside her (e.g., more careful of what she eats, drinks, activities, etc.)	As the Christian's assurance grows, he/she is more supportive of the new life inside (e.g., more careful of what he/she says, watches, reads, activities, etc.)

Just as a pregnant woman changes her behavior to support the new life growing inside her, as Christians we should change our behaviors (i.e., works) to support the new life inside us (James 2:14-26). Therefore, our _____ [10] should follow our _____ [11]. Just as a woman changes her behavior *because* she's pregnant and not in order to *become* pregnant, likewise a Christian's behavior should change *because* he or she is saved by faith, and not in order to *become* saved.

Is the level of your _____ [12] in your salvation equal to the level of your sincere works? This could be why in Romans 8:31-39 Paul overwhelmingly affirms our salvation—so that we would persevere in our faith with absolute assurance of salvation even during times of _____ [13].

> *How confident are you of your salvation? What behaviors did you change after you became a Christian? What current behaviors should you change to let your salvation be more evident?*

> Read the book of Romans one time in the week – two chapters per day (or as a stretch goal read it two times). What parts stood out to you the most? What unique characteristics about Christ does Paul describe? In what ways does this book help you to become more like Christ?

[1] future hope; [2] penalty of sin; [3] sin; [4] Jesus; [5] adopted; [6] sinful nature; [7] promise; [8] oath; [9] redemption; [10] works; [11] faith; [12] assurance; [13] suffering

Lesson 5: Moral Excellence

Lesson Summary
- As an internal discipline, moral excellence means being righteous or pure; if we were truly broken in repentance over our sin, then we should seek to purify our hearts in order to purify our behaviors.
- Though we will never be sinless, we should strive to sin less.
- God knows our innermost thoughts and desires. As we continue to humbly seek and set our minds on Him, His Spirit inside will empower us to live a life of righteousness that honors Him.

 **Bible Reading:** *Ephesians*
- Minimum Homework: Read the entire book twice (2 chapter per day)
- Stretch Goal: Read the entire book four times (4 chapters per day)

 Hymn: I Need Thee Every Hour
(written by Annie Hawkins, 1872)

I need Thee every hour, stay Thou nearby;
Temptations lose their power when Thou art nigh.

I need Thee every hour, in joy or pain;
Come quickly and abide, or life is in vain.

I need Thee, O I need Thee; Every hour I need Thee;
O bless me now, my Savior, I come to Thee.

 Hymn: Come Thou Fount Of Every Blessing
(written by Robert Robinson, 1758)

O to grace how great a debtor, Daily I'm constrained to be!
Let Thy goodness, like a fetter, Bind my wandering heart to Thee.
Prone to wander, Lord, I feel it, Prone to leave the God I love;
Here's my heart, O take and seal it, Seal it for Thy courts above.

Lesson 5: Moral Excellence

The next three internal disciplines
With a firm foundation of faith from the prior three lessons, the next three lessons cover the remaining internal disciplines: Moral Excellence, Knowledge and Self Control.

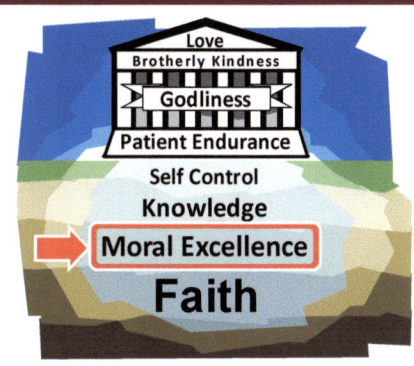

As internal disciplines, these aren't characteristics that can be seen or measured in ourselves or other Christians. Even so, each is very necessary for solidifying the foundation of faith on which our external disciplines can be seen by others. These next three disciplines help us to fulfill Jesus' greatest commandment (Deut 6:5; Mark 12:29-30) by aligning our heart, soul, mind and strength to our faith in Christ:

- Moral Excellence—Aligns our _____ [1] to our faith.
- Knowledge—Aligns our _____ [2] to our faith.
- Self Control—Aligns our _____ [3] to our faith.

What is moral excellence?
Several other versions of the Bible translate this as "virtue". It means being righteous, good, pure, undefiled—conforming your life to moral and ethical principles. It is an internal discipline to the faith on which it is founded; a resolute inspiration or commitment to avoid the very sin which that Christian had already repented of and was already forgiven for.

As discussed in the previous lessons, faith is the first step in our journey toward becoming like Christ. That faith is based on repenting of our sins and trusting in the death and resurrection of Jesus as the penalty for our sins so that we can be _____ [4] into God's family. If that is our foundation, then how can we continue in the very sin we repented of and that Jesus bore on our behalf? To do so is like building again the very wall that was torn down that had previously separated us from God.

Does this mean I should be sinless?
We will never **be sinless**, but we **should sin less**. Jesus is the only One that was sinless and therefore the only One qualified to be a _____ [5] for sin on our behalf. While we are on this side of Heaven, we will always be prone to temptation and sin. However, if God's Spirit abides within Christians, then we should live a life without sin that reflects His nature inside us.

 "My old self has been crucified with Christ. It is no longer I who live, but Christ lives in me. So I live in this earthly body by trusting in the Son of God, who loved me and gave Himself for me." (Galatians 2:20)

 *"This means that anyone who belongs to Christ has become a new person. The old life is gone; a new life has begun!" (2 Corinthians 5:17)*

If you are a Christian, then your old life of sin has died; you are a new person and are merely the "storage tank" for God's Spirit living inside.

But moral excellence is more than just doing what's right and sinning less. All of our actions originate as ideas or thoughts. Having moral excellence requires changing the way we think so that our Christ-like _____ [6] will lead to Christ-like _____ [7].

Lesson 5: Moral Excellence (continued)

 "Don't copy the behavior and customs of this world, but let God transform you into a new person by changing the way you think. Then you will learn to know God's will for you, which is good and pleasing and perfect." (Romans 12:2)

God is the One Who transforms Christians into new creations. He's done it spiritually through Christ's _____[8]. But He's also doing it this side of heaven when we yield our minds to Him to allow Him to change the way we think, and therefore our actions.

How did Jesus demonstrate moral excellence?
Jesus Himself is the perfect model for moral excellence. But as the Son of God, we wouldn't expect anything less from Him than to be completely sinless during His life on earth (2 Cor 5:21; Heb 4:15). But Jesus does more than model a life without sin.

Jesus holds us to a higher standard by addressing the place where the seed of sin germinates: _____ _____[9]. In so doing, He is ensuring our internal thoughts and motives are pure before God.

 *"You have heard that our ancestors were told, 'You must not murder. If you commit murder, you are subject to judgment.' But I say, if you are even angry with someone, you are subject to judgment! ...You have heard the commandment that says, 'You must not commit adultery.' But I say, anyone who even looks at a woman with lust has already committed adultery with her in his heart." (Matthew 5:21-22, 27-28)*

Jesus is saying that stopping the physical act of sin is not enough. Sin originates in our hearts and God will judge us based on our heart motives—even if we didn't outwardly act on those sinful desires.

If we're already guilty for the sin we commit in our heart, then why not act on it anyway? Such foolish logic only reveals the person's real sinful motives. Even so, acting upon that sin is still very different and more harmful, as we'll review more in depth as we study the discipline of godliness in Lesson 9. Jesus' point was that all sin _____[10] in the heart. If we've truly repented of our sins and wish to stop sinning, then we must confront the thoughts and motives of our heart.

 *"For the word of God is alive and powerful. It is sharper than the sharpest two-edged sword, cutting between soul and spirit, between joint and marrow. It exposes our innermost thoughts and desires. Nothing in all creation is hidden from God. Everything is naked and exposed before His eyes, and He is the One to whom we are accountable." (Hebrews 4:12-13)*

We may easily deceive our family and friends about our control over sin, but only God sees our "innermost thoughts and desires". If we really knew how much God sees directly into our hearts, then would we be more willing to pursue Christ-like thoughts that will lead us to Christ-like behavior?

 How often and how deeply have you thought about how God sees every motive of your heart? If you were more aware of this, would it change your thoughts or behaviors? Why or why not?

What did other Christians in church history teach about moral excellence?
All Christians in church history have struggled with sin to varying degrees after they became a Christian. If this weren't true, then there wouldn't have been such strong exhortation by New Testament authors

Lesson 5: Moral Excellence (continued)

(i.e., Paul, Peter, John, etc.) to encourage believers (both new and mature) to not sin. Below are a few of those passages that encourage us to _____[11] from sin and _____[12] moral excellence:

"Since you have heard about Jesus and have learned the truth that comes from Him, throw off your old sinful nature and your former way of life, which is corrupted by lust and deception. Instead, let the Spirit renew your thoughts and attitudes. Put on your new nature, created to be like God—truly righteous and holy." (Ephesians 4:21-24)

"Since you have been raised to new life with Christ, set your sights on the realities of heaven, where Christ sits in the place of honor at God's right hand. Think about the things of heaven, not the things of earth. For you died to this life, and your real life is hidden with Christ in God...Put on your new nature, and be renewed as you learn to know your Creator and become like Him." (Colossians 3:1-3,10)

"...Fix your thoughts on what is true, and honorable, and right, and pure, and lovely, and admirable. Think about things that are excellent and worthy of praise." (Philippians 4:8)

"We know that our old sinful selves were crucified with Christ so that sin might lose its power in our lives. We are no longer slaves to sin. For when we died with Christ we were set free from the power of sin...Do not let sin control the way you live; do not give in to sinful desires. Do not let any part of your body become an instrument of evil to serve sin. Instead, give yourselves completely to God, for you were dead, but now you have new life. So use your whole body as an instrument to do what is right for the glory of God." (Romans 6:6-7, 12-13)

Who would buy a sports car just to always drive 25 MPH? People who buy a sports car want to feel the power of quick acceleration to speeds much higher than 25 MPH. In the same way, Paul assures us in Romans 6 how Jesus' resurrection is proof that we are no longer under the power or control of sin. His Spirit in us empowers us to live a life of _____[13] for God's glory. Yet, why are we often unwilling to believe in and act on the power to "spiritually accelerate" for God's glory?

Perhaps it requires transforming what we know and how we think not only about who we are in Christ, but Who Christ is in us. We'll explore that more in our next internal discipline about Knowledge.

Do you sometimes feel like you are under the power or control of sin? What are some ways you could grow more confident in knowing you're free from the power of sin?

Read the book of Ephesians two times in the week – two chapters per day (or as a stretch goal read it four times). What parts stood out to you the most? What unique characteristics about Christ does Paul describe? In what ways does this book help you to become more like Christ?

[1] heart; [2] head; [3] hands; [4] adopted; [5] sacrifice; [6] thoughts; [7] behavior; [8] atonement; [9] our heart; [10] originates; [11] turn; [12] pursue; [13] righteousness

Lesson 6: Knowledge

Lesson Summary
- In this context, knowledge means growing in our understanding of God to love Him with all our mind.
- God Himself is our primary source for knowledge. When we seek Him first through a relationship, He will give us understanding about Himself, most often through, and never in contradiction to, His Word.
- Growing in a right knowledge of God can help protect us from false teachings and keep us grounded in our faith in Christ, as it has done for many Christians in history like Peter, Stephen, and Martin Luther.

Bible Reading: *2 Peter and 1 Timothy*
- Minimum Homework: Read each entire book two times (2 chapter per day)
- Stretch Goal: Read each entire book four times (4 chapters per day)

Hymn: The Lord Is In His Holy Place
(written by Nikolai F. S. Grundtvig, <1872)

So hear and heed His faithful Word, And trust His promise long,
For they who seek Him life shall find, And shall in Him be strong;
We need a perfect faith in Him, With understanding never dim,
To fill our daily lives with song.

Hymn: Give Me, O Lord, Right Views Of Thee
(written by Henry Putnam, >1861)

Give me, O Lord, right views of Thee, Thy glorious nature, love, and might;
And draw my spirit's eyes to see the things concealed from mortal sight;
And in the soul which Thou hast wrought, O breathe the understanding thought.

Give me, O Lord, right views of truth; Thy all discerning Spirit give,
To bring light in earliest youth Thy living words by which men live;
Of all Thy gifts, I pray, impart a wise and understanding heart.

Lesson 6: Knowledge

What is knowledge?

It's more than just "knowing" something. It's understanding something to the point where it influences how you think and what you believe.

For example, someone who wants to become a great chef will spend the majority of their time reading about cooking techniques, observing master chefs, learning the chemistry of flavor from different ingredients, etc. In essence, if becoming a chef is a priority, then they will spend their time and money to increase their knowledge and understanding of cooking until it becomes second nature to them.

In the same way, if our faith in Christ is a priority for us, then we should look for ways to grow in our knowledge and understanding about that faith. Just as with cooking, it requires using many resources to learn about that faith, such as _____[1], observing _____[2] in Christ (those we know personally or from history), and applying what we learn through on-going _____[3] with other believers.

What is our Primary Source for Knowledge?

Hint: It's NOT the Bible. Many people may be surprised that the Bible isn't our primary source for growing in our knowledge of our faith in Christ. Our primary source is actually God Himself.

 *"I pray for you constantly, asking God, the glorious Father of our Lord Jesus Christ, to give you spiritual wisdom and insight so that you might grow in your knowledge of God. I pray that your hearts will be flooded with light so that you can understand the confident hope He has given to those He called..." (Ephesians 1:16-18)*

 *"We ask God to give you complete knowledge of His will and to give you spiritual wisdom and understanding. Then the way you live will always honor and please the Lord, and your lives will produce every kind of good fruit. All the while, you will grow as you learn to know God better and better." (Colossians 1:9-10)*

 *"...God revealed these things by His Spirit. For His Spirit searches out everything and shows us God's deep secrets. ...no one can know God's thoughts except God's own Spirit. And we have received God's Spirit (not the world's spirit), so we can know the wonderful things God has freely given us." (1 Corinthians 2:11-12)*

If you wanted to learn how to paint, would you prefer to get private lessons from a master painter, or read a book about painting written by that master painter? Naturally, learning directly from a _____[4] with the master is the best way to learn and grow. Likewise, God is the primary source to grow in our faith since He is the very One in Whom our faith is founded.

Does this mean the Bible should not be a source for Knowledge?

Absolutely not! We only know that God is our primary source for knowledge about our faith because the Bible clearly states it. However, it is important to understand that although the

Lesson 6: Knowledge (continued)

Bible is very critical to growing in our knowledge of our faith, it is merely a tool that helps us grow by pointing us to our primary source: _____ [5].

As we learned in Lesson 2, God reveals Himself to humanity in a "special" way through His commands. A broader form of this special revelation is through the Bible. The Bible is filled with many stories that we teach to children in Sunday School, like Noah's ark, Moses & Pharaoh, Joshua at Jericho, David & Goliath, Daniel & the lion's den, etc. These are such wonderful stories, but God didn't give us these stories to tell us how wonderful Noah, Moses, Joshua, David, and Daniel are. In every story God Himself is the _____ [6] to demonstrate His awesome love for and power through His people.

The Bible is our Secondary Source for Knowledge

As the timeline below illustrates, before the time of Christ God's people grew in their knowledge about their faith through stories, then through the Law, and eventually through the additional writings that make up the Old Testament. In the first century, God revealed Himself to His people through Jesus which they expressed through their own writings which make up the New Testament.

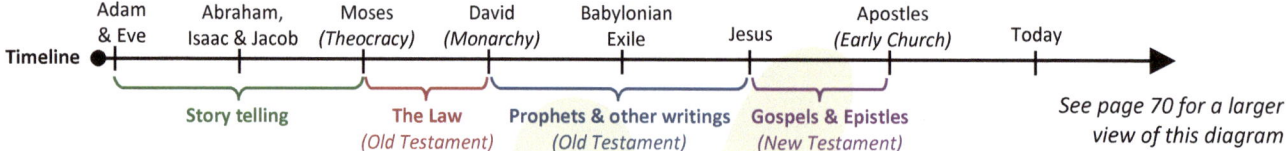

See page 70 for a larger view of this diagram

Even though this is how God has created His inspired Word (our Bible) over time, it is still only a tool that points us to His most inspired and living Word: _____ [7].

"Long ago God spoke many times and in many ways to our ancestors through the prophets. And now in these final days, He has spoken to us through His Son." (Hebrews 1:1-2)

"In the beginning the Word already existed. The Word was with God, and the Word was God. He existed in the beginning with God." (John 1:1-2)

So, should we directly seek God for knowledge *instead of* using the Bible? Of course not! We need to primarily seek God for knowledge (John 6:45) and one of the best ways He has _____ [8] us to do that is through His inspired written Word, the Bible.

"You have been taught the holy Scriptures from childhood, and they have given you the wisdom to receive the salvation that comes by trusting in Christ Jesus. All Scripture is inspired by God and is useful to teach us what is true and make us realize what is wrong in our lives. It corrects us when we are wrong and teaches us to do what is right. God uses it to prepare and equip His people to do every good work." (2 Timothy 3:15-17)

As you read the Bible to seek God, it's critical to ensure you read and interpret it correctly. Taking it out of context (even with good intentions) is a form of taking the Lord's _____ [9]. Why? Because it's claiming God said or meant something that He never actually intended (2 Peter 3:15-17). Lesson 12 describes in more detail how to properly interpret and apply scripture to our daily lives.

How did Jesus demonstrate knowledge?

As the Son of God, Jesus had an undeniable relationship with the Father to grow in knowledge in His human life. Even so, Jesus demonstrated many times His knowledge of _____ [10] to combat those who tried to attack Him. For example, in Matthew 4 when Jesus was being tempted by the devil, Jesus quoted scripture each time to defend His reason why He would not yield to temptation.

Lesson 6: Knowledge (continued)

In verse 6, Satan even tried to use scripture as part of the temptation, but again Jesus would not yield because He had a deeper and more accurate knowledge of the truth of scripture.

"The people were amazed at His teaching, for He taught with real authority—quite unlike the teachers of religious law" (Mark 1:22)

We can presume that the teachers and Pharisees in Jesus' day were very familiar with Scripture, but they used it as an end instead of as a means to reach the ultimate end, _____ [11].

"What sorrow awaits you teachers of the religious law and you Pharisees. Hypocrites! For you are careful to tithe even the tiniest income from your herb gardens, but you ignore the more important aspects of the law—justice, mercy, and faith. You should tithe, yes, but do not neglect the more important things." (Matthew 23:23)

In addition, many other passages show how Jesus knew scripture intimately and effectively applied it: Matthew 11:10, Matthew 12:3-8, Matthew 22:36-46, Mark 12:10-11, Luke 4:17-22, Luke 24:44-47, John 7:21-38, John 8:17, John 10:34-35, John 13:18, and John 17:12.

How did other Christians in church history demonstrate knowledge?

In the early church, Peter demonstrated his knowledge and application of scripture as he preached the gospel in Acts 2:16-35, 3:22-26, 4:11-26. As well, Acts 6 & 7 describe the story of _____ [12] who was known to be full of God's grace and wisdom even though he was probably a young believer. He proved his deep knowledge of scripture during his defense before the Jewish High Council.

Over the next 1500 years, the Church had evolved to the point where church leaders were selling "good works" (called indulgences) from a so-called treasury in heaven built up by Jesus, the apostles, and saints. This, along with many other unbiblical doctrines, were widely taught in the Church and commonly believed by its followers. But while seeking God through the scriptures, a German monk named _____ [13] read Romans 1:17 that "the just shall live by faith". This passage sparked his desire to search the scriptures more to understand God's justification by faith. As a result, on October 31, 1517 he posted to the door of the Church at Wittenberg his famous Ninety-Five Theses which publicly denounced many of the unbiblical teachings and practices in the Church. This helped ignite the Protestant _____ [14], arguably the most significant event for the Church ever since the 1st century church.

Describe a time where if you had the knowledge then that you have now, it could have changed the situation. How would things be different now if you had a deeper knowledge of God?

Read 2 Peter & 1 Timothy two times in the week – two chapters per day (or as a stretch goal read them four times). What parts stood out to you the most? What unique characteristics about Christ do they describe? In what ways do these books help you to become more like Christ?

[1] reading the Bible; [2] mature believers; [3] fellowship; [4] relationship; [5] God Himself; [6] central character; [7] Jesus Christ; [8] enabled; [9] name in vain; [10] scripture; [11] God Himself; [12] Stephen; [13] Martin Luther; [14] Reformation

Lesson 7: Self-Control

Lesson Summary
- As a gatekeeper to our hearts and minds, self-control's first function is to filter what comes INTO us; fasting food or other pleasures is a practical way to build self-control over the things that come into us.
- The second function of self-control is to filter what goes OUT from us, such as through our words; giving our money, time, or other resources is a practical way to build self-control over what goes out from us.
- When we don't use self-control in our words or actions, we should closely examine why and what it reveals about possible sin hidden in our heart; in those times, we must pray and surrender it to Christ.

Bible Reading: *James*
- Minimum Homework: Read the entire book twice (2 chapter per day)
- Stretch Goal: Read the entire book four times (4 chapters per day)

Hymn: O Kind Creator, Bend Thine Ear
(written by Gregory I, 6th century)

Our hearts are open, Lord, to Thee; Thou knowest our infirmity;
Pour out on all who seek Thy face abundance of Thy pardoning grace.

Our sins are many, this we know; Spare us, good Lord, Thy mercy show;
And for the honor of Thy Name our fainting souls to life reclaim.

Give us the self control that springs from discipline of outward things,
That fasting inward secretly the soul may purely dwell with Thee.

We pray Thee, Holy Trinity, One God, unchanging Unity,
That we from this our abstinence may reap the fruits of penitence.

Lesson 7: Self-Control

What is self-control?
Also known as "temperance", self-control is restraining our feelings or desires that might lead us to sinful or undesirable behaviors. As the last of the internal disciplines, it is like their outer layer and serves as a _____[1] to our heart and mind to perform two basic functions:

1. **Filters what comes INTO us**
   (the external influences we absorb internally)

2. **Filters what goes OUT from us**
   (the treasures of our heart we express externally)

See page 68 for a larger view of this diagram

Function 1: Filtering what comes INTO us
What is your most precious earthly treasure? What do you do to protect it? For example, if you have kids, do you protect them by ensuring they have food and shelter, that they're in good health, and that they aren't exposed to danger?

Generally, people will try to protect and care for the earthly things they value. In the same way, if we value the _____[2] of our souls, then we should also make every effort to protect it. Self-control is that vigilant guard at the gates of our heart and mind that helps ensure the other internal disciplines (our faith, moral excellence, and knowledge of God) remain strong and _____[3] sound.

How do we enforce this protection from external influences?
If a thief broke into your home, then the next time you leave your home would you leave your doors and windows unlocked? Most people would not, and in fact they may even install some extra protection to prevent future robberies. In the same way, our sinful failures should be an _____[4] for us to recognize when we did not exercise proper self-control.

Generally, sin isn't an instantaneous act. It's nearly always something we're led into like yielding to temptation, harboring unforgiveness, wandering from _____[5] with God or other Christians, etc. If we're humble before God and honest with ourselves, we will probably recall some of the warning signs we ignored before we sinned. When that occurs, ask yourself:
- What warning signs did I ignore that could've prevented me from sinning?
- Why did I ignore those warning signs?
- What safeguards can I use to ensure I don't ignore those warning signs and yield to sin?

 *"So if your eye...causes you to lust, gouge it out and throw it away...if your hand...causes you to sin, cut it off and throw it away. It is better for you to lose one part of your body than for your whole body to be thrown into hell." (Matthew 5:29-30)*

Nearly all theologians agree that Jesus is speaking figuratively in this passage. Even so, He's saying this to illustrate how serious sin is and that we should use _____[6] to prevent future sin. Aside from gouging out our eyes or cutting off our hands, some other

Lesson 7: Self-Control (continued)

drastic measures to prevent sin include:
- Extend your devotional time with God (continue to seek brokenness over the sin).
- Confess your sin to your spouse or a trusted Christian friend and be _____[7] to them.
- Cut off the source of temptation (e.g., wrong relationships, the internet, cable TV, etc.).

Fasting - a secondary discipline for filtering what comes INTO us

Jesus describes the discipline of fasting during His Sermon on the Mount (Matthew 6:16-18). Fasting implies more than just temporarily abstaining from food, but in our culture it could include other things that bring pleasure like television, internet, sports, music, etc. Although there may not be anything inherently wrong with these, temporarily abstaining from them helps curb our _____[8] for earthly pleasures. When we do that, it's good to fill that time instead with spiritual things, like prayer.

What other extreme safeguards (e.g., cutting off your hand) could you use to guarantee self-control? If those are unrealistic, then what practical, yet effective ways could you use instead?

Function 2: Filtering what goes OUT from us

As good as it is to filter the external things that influence us internally, it is just as important to use self-control to filter our internal thoughts, desires and motivations that we express _____[9].

"For whatever is in your heart determines what you say. A good person produces good things from the treasury of a good heart, and an evil person produces evil things from the treasury of an evil heart." (Matthew 12:34-35)

"But the words you speak come from the heart—that's what defiles you. For from the heart come evil thoughts, murder, adultery, all sexual immorality, theft, lying, and slander." (Matthew 15:18-19)

In response to religious leaders who challenged Him, Jesus' statements above prove that our words and actions reflect who we are inside. If we are Christians who are declared to be righteous by faith in Jesus and diligently seek the other internal disciplines of moral excellence and knowledge, then that is what our words and actions should reflect. We need self-control to prevent us from using words or actions that contradict our _____[10] with and _____[11] to Christ.

How do we enforce self-control over our words and actions?

Just like with external influences, we need to watch for warning signs and employ safeguards when we outwardly express our thoughts or feelings. This includes guarding our words and asking ourselves:
- What warning signs did I ignore (and why) that could've prevented me from saying or doing that?
- What safeguards can I use to ensure I don't ignore those warning signs and yield to sin?
- Most importantly, what do my wrong words and actions _____[12] about who I truly am at heart?

Based on Jesus' statements above, if we find our words and actions to be ungodly, then is that evidence that we are harboring evil intentions in our heart? At those times we should pray and thoroughly examine ourselves according to the 3 prior internal disciplines:
- *FAITH* - What area of my life have I not repented of and totally surrendered to Christ? (2 Cor 13:5)
- *MORAL* EXCELLENCE - What hidden part of me does God see and want _____[13]? (Eph 4:21-24)
- *KNOWLEDGE* - What does God's Word say about this issue and how I should deal with it? (Col 3:1-3)

Lesson 7: Self-Control (continued)

Giving - a secondary discipline for filtering what goes OUT from us

Jesus describes the discipline of giving during His Sermon on the Mount (Matthew 6:1-4, 19-24). Giving implies more than just money, but also our time and other resources. If we've given our lives to Christ as believers, then that means 100% of all we have belongs to Him - not just 10% (i.e., the tithe). We are merely _____[14] of all He has given us. By practicing the discipline of giving, we are exercising self-control over what goes out from us and may further help us control our words and behaviors.

How did Jesus demonstrate self-control?

Although Jesus faced the same temptations we do, He exercised self-control and never sinned.

"This High Priest of ours understands our weaknesses, for He faced all of the same testings we do, yet He did not sin. (Hebrews 4:15)

An example of this is in Matthew 4:1-11 when Jesus was tempted by Satan in the wilderness. Despite the three temptations recorded in the passage, Jesus used self-control and never yielded to them.

In a similar way, Jesus used self-control while in the garden of Gethsemane (Matthew 26:36-44). Though it doesn't explicitly say they were temptations like in Matthew 4, they were desires Jesus expressed (by asking for the cup of suffering to pass) that He knew was in conflict with His Father's will. But He did not yield to humanly desires, but _____[15] the Father and _____[16] the cross for us.

How did other Christians in church history demonstrate self-control?

The New Testament doesn't give many specific examples of self-control exercised by early church leaders. Even so, it was understood to be practiced and preached, even to the point where Paul mandated self-control not only as a _____[17] for elders in the church, but for their wives too.

"So an elder must be a man whose life is above reproach...He must exercise self-control, live wisely, and have a good reputation...In the same way, their wives...must exercise self-control and be faithful in everything they do." (1 Timothy 3:2,11)

"So think clearly and exercise self-control...So you must live as God's obedient children. Don't slip back into your old ways of living to satisfy your own desires. You didn't know any better then. But now you must be holy in everything you do, just as God who chose you is holy. For the Scriptures say, 'You must be holy because I am holy.'" (1 Peter 1:13-16)

In what ways do you need more self-control over the external things that influence you? In what ways do you need it for things that come out of you, like your words or behaviors?

Read the book of James two times in the week – two chapters per day (or as a stretch goal read it four times). What parts stood out to you the most? What unique characteristics about Christ does James describe? In what ways does this book help you to become more like Christ?

[1] gatekeeper; [2] eternal salvation; [3] biblically; [4] opportunity; [5] fellowship; [6] drastic measures; [7] accountable; [8] appetite; [9] outwardly; [10] relationship; [11] allegiance; [12] reveal; [13] purified; [14] stewards; [15] obeyed; [16] embraced; [17] requirement

Lesson 8: Patient Endurance

Lesson Summary
- Patient endurance should be what others see in us when we are "squeezed" by adversity and suffering.
- Our spirituality isn't measured by the frequency or severity of our suffering, but by our response to it; the more deeply we sail in our faith in Christ, the less affected our faith is when we encounter adversity.
- When we are a victim of adversity, we need to cling more tightly to Christ; when others are victims, we need to support them if we can and be thankful for God's mercy that we are not the victims ourselves.

 **Bible Reading:** *1 Peter*
- Minimum Homework: Read the entire book three times (2 chapter per day)
- Stretch Goal: Read the entire book four times (3 chapters per day)

 Hymn: It Is Well With My Soul
(written by Horatio P. Spafford, 1873)

When peace, like a river, attendeth my way, When sorrows like sea billows roll;
Whatever my lot, Thou has taught me to say, It is well, it is well, with my soul.

Though Satan should buffet, though trials should come, Let this blest assurance control,
That Christ has regarded my helpless estate, And hath shed His own blood for my soul.

My sin, oh, the bliss of this glorious thought! My sin, not in part but the whole,
Is nailed to the cross, and I bear it no more, Praise the Lord, praise the Lord, O my soul!

For me, be it Christ, be it Christ hence to live: If Jordan above me shall roll,
No pang shall be mine, for in death as in life Thou wilt whisper Thy peace to my soul.

And Lord, haste the day when my faith shall be sight, The clouds be rolled back as a scroll;
The trump shall resound, and the Lord shall descend, Even so, it is well with my soul.

Lesson 8: Patient Endurance

What is patient endurance?

The Bible also describes this as "perseverance". It means to remain steadfast, unwavering, and _____ [1] in what you believe or know. The context from scripture describes it as working hard to pursue the course set before us without becoming distracted or entangled by evil opposition.

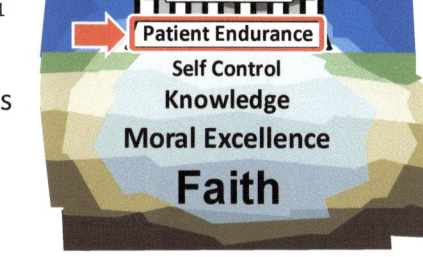

As the first of the external disciplines, patient endurance serves as the wide _____ [2] on which is standing the remaining external disciplines of godliness, brotherly kindness and love. It can be the first and most visible of the external disciplines, especially when it's amidst suffering.

Suffering? Isn't Christianity supposed to keep me from suffering?

Absolutely not. In fact, Christians should expect suffering:

"Dear brothers and sisters, when troubles come your way, consider it an opportunity for great joy. For you know that when your faith is tested, your endurance has a chance to grow. So let it grow, for when your endurance is fully developed, you will be perfect and complete, needing nothing." (James 1:2-4)

"We can rejoice, too, when we run into problems and trials, for we know that they help us develop endurance. And endurance develops strength of character, and character strengthens our confident hope of salvation." (Romans 5:3-4)

These passages state "when", not "if", we encounter troubles. But Paul even calls it a privilege:

"For you have been given not only the privilege of trusting in Christ but also the privilege of suffering for Him." (Philippians 1:29)

How can suffering be a privilege? Aren't Christians supposed to have peace?

Peace is one of the fruits of the Spirit described in Galatians 5:22-23. Just as juice comes out when you squeeze an orange, peace should come out as a _____ [3] of the Holy Spirit (Who resides within us) when Christians get spiritually "squeezed" by adversity.

We have peace with God because He set us free from His death penalty by substituting it with the atoning death of Jesus (lessons 2 and 3). This foundation of faith (the first and foremost discipline for becoming like Christ) has _____ [4] the fellowship we had once broken with God and thereby making us at peace with Him. As a result, we can have assurance of our salvation because God placed His Spirit in us as a seal for the resurrection all Christians can confidently hope for (lesson 4). That confidence is the _____ [5] to help us endure during times of adversity (Hebrews 6:18-19).

Unfortunately, many professing Christians are like the rocky soil Jesus described in His parable of the soils (Matthew 13:20-21); they fell away during difficult times perhaps because they expected Christianity to give them a happy, trouble-free life. Christians will never be immune to suffering, but are simply able to endure it with God's peace. Suffering is a reliable way to test if we have His peace. Therefore, suffering is a way for others to see the _____ [6] of our internal disciplines (faith, moral excellence, knowledge and self-control).

Lesson 8: Patient Endurance (continued)

How to survive a tsunami of suffering

A tsunami is a huge tidal wave generally caused by an earthquake in the middle of the ocean. Just like throwing a rock in a pool of water, the rippling waves from the energy of the earthquake extend outward until they reach land. When the water is deep, the waves may only be a few feet high and hardly noticeable by anyone out at sea. As the wave approaches shore where the water is more shallow, it forces the water upward to create a massive, destructive wave.

In the same way, the deeper Christians go in their faith in Christ is like going into deeper waters, while those who are shallow in their faith may be like those in shallow water near the shoreline. When adversity comes (like an earthquake), those in deeper waters are _____[7]. But those near the shoreline are most _____[8] to the destructive impact from the rising waves of adversity.

① The faith of Christians in "deep water" is unaffected by waves.

② Professing Christians in "shallow water" are most vulnerable to waves.

③ Since Non-Christians have no saving faith, the waves of suffering won't affect them spiritually.

How Tsunamis Occur:
❶ Earthquake in ocean floor
❷ Energy from earthquake causes rippling waves that are very small in deep water.
❸ Shallow ground near the shore forces water upward to make enormous waves.

See page 69 for a larger view of this diagram

Whose fault is it for all the suffering?

When we are the victim of adversity, it's common to ask "Why?" and look for a cause and effect; that way if we find a cause, then maybe we can prevent those effects from happening again. It's usually obvious to us when our adversity is a _____[9] of the sin or actions from ourselves or others. But often times it may just be the result of natural circumstances occurring in our fallen world.

Some Christians, who are not the victims of adversity themselves, tend to "blame" God. That is, they may assume He's judging those victims for their sins like He did at times in the Old Testament. However, without direct _____[10] from God (like they had in those same Old Testament examples), any such assumptions are unfounded and may impede the spread of the gospel.

Our spirituality isn't measured by the frequency or severity of our suffering, but by our _____[11] to it. Jesus implied this for three separate tragedies:
- John 9:1-3 - Blindness was neither due to the sin of the man nor his parents.
- Luke 13:1-2 - Murder of the Galileans wasn't due to their sin.
- Luke 13:3-4 - Tower of Siloam that fell on 18 people wasn't due to their sin.

In each example, Jesus clearly stated their suffering wasn't due to sin, and was more concerned about the response (fruit) from the suffering. This doesn't mean that God will never use tragedy to judge people for sins, but it should certainly _____[12] us from being too impetuous about attributing it to God.

Rather than searching for a reason for suffering, we should be thankful for God's mercy when we are not the victims. And when we are the victim, we need to seize it as an _____[13] to lean on Christ so that we can be more like Him by identifying with His sufferings for us. It's in those times we need to patiently endure them by clinging more tightly and sailing more _____[14] in our faith in Christ.

Lesson 8: Patient Endurance (continued)

How did Jesus demonstrate patient endurance?
Jesus is clearly our perfect example of patient endurance as most clearly seen through the torture and execution He endured for our _____[15]. But He demonstrated it in many other ways such as:
- Matthew 4:1-11 - Jesus endured the temptations from Satan in the wilderness.
- Matthew 8:23-27 - Jesus calmed a storm with just His word.
- Matthew 12:22-37 - Religious leaders accuse Jesus that His power is from Satan.
- Luke 4:16-30 - Jesus is rejected by His hometown of Nazareth where they attempt to kill Him.
- John 7:1-9 - Jesus' brothers ridicule Him and His ministry.
- Luke 20:1-8, 20-40 - Jesus is challenged by the religious leaders.
- Luke 22:3-6, 54-65 - Jesus is betrayed by a close friend (Judas) and denied by His closest friend (Peter).

How did other Christians in church history demonstrate patient endurance?
Although Jesus is our perfect example of patient endurance, we can look to other fellow Christians for encouragement of how to endure our own adversities with patience - even to the point of martyrdom. Peter was the central figure for the early church. He endured persecution, scourging and imprisonment from the religious leaders on several occasions, yet continued to faithfully preach the gospel (Acts 4:1-22, 5:17-42, 12:1-5). His own endurance became a _____[16] that underscored his message to many churches in his first epistle (1 Peter) that they should also patiently endure suffering.

Paul is arguably the most prominent early Church example of patient endurance. Ironically, he was also one of the foremost persecutors of the early church (Acts 7:60-8:3, 9:1-2) until his dramatic conversion (Acts 9:3-19). He endured death threats (Acts 9:23-25, 23:12-31), rejection (Acts 13:50-14:7), stonings (Acts 14:19-20), beatings (Acts 16:22-23), imprisonment (Acts 16:23-34, 21:26-36), a shipwreck (Acts 27), etc. In 2 Corinthians 11:18-12:10, he recounts the various adversities he faced in his life. Yet he _____[17] and took _____[18] in these knowing it's due to the power of Christ working though him.

Church history is filled with many other examples of Christians who patiently endured adversity, such as Ignatius, Polycarp, Justin Martyr, Irenaeus, Tertullian, Origen, Athanasius, John Wycliffe, Martin Luther, etc. Despite these hardships, their lives continue to echo Paul's sentiment:

> "We patiently endure troubles and hardships and calamities of every kind...We prove ourselves by our purity, our understanding, our patience, our kindness, by the Holy Spirit in us, and by our sincere love....We serve God whether people honor us or despise us..." (2 Corinthians 6:3-10)

Read 2 Corinthians 4:7-17. How do you normally react when you're "squeezed" by adversity? What can you do to align your attitude with Paul's Christ-centered example during adversity?

Read the book of 1 Peter three times in the week – two chapters per day (or as a stretch goal read it four times). What parts stood out to you the most? What unique characteristics about Christ does Peter describe? In what ways does this book help you to become more like Christ?

[1] consistent; [2] platform; [3] natural byproduct; [4] restored; [5] anchor; [6] depth; [7] unaffected; [8] vulnerable; [9] consequence; [10] revelation; [11] response; [12] prevent; [13] opportunity; [14] deeply; [15] atonement; [16] living proof; [17] boasted; [18] pleasure

Lesson 9: Godliness

Lesson Summary
- Jesus used the parables of The Good Samaritan and The Sheep And The Goats to teach how godliness is most visible when Christians show compassion by serving others who are going through adversity.
- If we're on the job or serving at church, we ultimately work for Christ and should do it with excellence.
- Godliness is not a choice based on how we feel; it's based on our commitment to serve and honor Christ in all we do - even if that means not engaging in behaviors that we think won't affect others.

Bible Reading: *1 Corinthians*
- Minimum Homework: Read the entire book one time (2 chapters per day)
- Stretch Goal: Read the entire book two times (4 chapters per day)

Hymn: O To Be Like Thee
(written by Thomas O. Chisholm, 1897)

O to be like Thee! Blessed Redeemer, this is my constant longing and prayer;
Gladly I'll forfeit all of earth's treasures, Jesus, Thy perfect likeness to wear.

O to be like Thee! O to be like Thee, Blessed Redeemer, pure as Thou art;
Come in Thy sweetness, come in Thy fullness; stamp Thine own image deep on my heart.

O to be like Thee! Full of compassion, loving, forgiving, tender and kind,
Helping the helpless, cheering the fainting, seeking the wandering sinner to find.

O to be like Thee! Lowly in spirit, holy and harmless, patient and brave;
Meekly enduring cruel reproaches, willing to suffer others to save.

O to be like Thee! Lord, I am coming now to receive anointing divine;
All that I am and have I am bringing, Lord, from this moment all shall be Thine.

O to be like Thee! While I am pleading, pour out Thy Spirit, fill with Thy love;
Make me a temple meet for Thy dwelling, fit me for life and heaven above.

Lesson 9: Godliness

What is godliness?

Godliness is not just acting godly in the same way we may ask ourselves "what would Jesus do?" The Bible implies that godliness means demonstrating a reverence, respect or piety toward God as reflected in our behavior. More simply, it's asking "what would _____[1] Jesus?"

How does godliness differ from patient endurance?

Although patient endurance is the first external discipline visible by others, it's generally seen in our response to the adversity that we face. In contrast, godliness is what others may see as our response to adversity that _____[2] face.

*When we face adversity, others see our **patient endurance**:*

*When we help others facing adversity, they see our **godliness**:*

When others face adversity, Christians or Christian ministries are often among the first ones to give and offer help, such as when towns are struck by natural disasters, feeding the hungry, clothing the naked, caring for orphans, etc. It is a response of _____[3] to help the helpless as mandated and demonstrated by God Himself throughout the Bible.

Read Matthew 25:31-46. In this famous passage, Jesus states that when we show compassion to our brothers and sisters in need, it's as if we were doing it to Him. As the One judging all of these people, He _____[4] them (and us as Christians) to show this kind of godly service to others; it's not a choice. It's interesting to note that in v. 37—40, the righteous ones didn't even realize they were doing their godly service unto Jesus; instead it was a natural _____[5] of who they were as devoted followers of Christ.

Don't I have to be a preacher or missionary to do all these godly things?

No. Many missionaries do care for others in dramatic ways (like in Jesus' example by feeding the hungry, clothing the naked, caring for the sick, etc.), Jesus expects us to care for others in that way to our _____[6]—whether that's across the globe or across the street.

Read Luke 10:25-37, the passage of the Good Samaritan. The man asked Jesus "Who is my neighbor?" as if trying to understand who should receive the compassion he's expected to show. But after telling the parable, Jesus asks him which person "was a neighbor to the man who was attacked?" By asking this, it seems Jesus' point is that a neighbor is the one _____[7] compassion and not the one _____[8] it. Although God is very concerned for those in need, He is just as concerned for those who are serving others out of compassion.

What are other ways can we show godliness?

If as Christians we have truly surrendered our lives to Christ, then all of our actions should

Lesson 9: Godliness (continued)

reflect that submission and honor to Him. Perhaps the degree of our _____ [9] to Christ can be measured by how much our lives _____ [10] Him. Since godliness is an external discipline, this would especially apply to all of our actions that are visible by others. This means more than while at church or showing compassion to others in need, but can also apply to our everyday work ethic.

How do I show godliness at work?

It's not about acting "godly" at work. Paul instructs slaves to have deep respect and fear for their masters. Today we can apply those same principles to an employee/employer relationship.

> "Serve them sincerely as you would serve Christ. Try to please them all the time, not just when they are watching you. As slaves of Christ, do the will of God with all your heart. Work with enthusiasm, as though you were working for the Lord rather than for people." (Ephesians 6:5-8)

So our perspective should be that we are working for Christ, and not just our employer. With Christ as the One we ultimately serve, we need to ask "what would honor Jesus" in all that we do such as when we talk to or about those we work with. We need to be truthful, respectful in our attitudes, faithful to our commitments (like arriving on time), and diligent to pursue excellence with the same _____ [11] as if we did it for Christ. Paul even expects the same attitude from those in authority (v. 9).

Paul doesn't say this only applies when you like or agree with your employer. Peter is even more explicit:

> "You...must accept the authority of your masters with all respect. Do what they tell you-not only if they are kind and reasonable, but even if they are cruel. For God is pleased with you when you do what you know is right and patiently endure unfair treatment." (1 Peter 2:18-19)

Would your co-workers consider your behavior at work to be godly? Why or why not?

If this is what's expected of us when we work for others (including non-Christians), how much more should we have that same Christ-centered work ethic when we serve in our local church? The fact that we may be volunteers in ministry should not change our pursuit of _____ [12] in all things from preaching or leading music all the way down to scrubbing toilets or changing diapers in the nursery. It's not the work we're performing that matters, but Who we're performing it for: Christ.

What about godly behaviors that don't affect others?

What about drinking alcohol, smoking, dancing, or gambling? These are examples of behaviors that don't always affect others. Why are they often considered forbidden by many Christians?

There is wide disparity among Christians on whether or not behaviors like these are appropriate for Christians. Although it's not the intent of this Discipleship Guide to review each of these behaviors in detail, Lesson 10 (the discipline of Brotherly Kindness) addresses the attitude Christians should have for behaviors like these that are hotly debated. Even so, when you face questionable behavior, there are four questions you could ask yourself to understand if it is permissible:

1. Does the Bible explicitly _____ [13] the behavior or call it a sin? (See Lesson 12)
2. Could the behavior open a door of temptation for me to sin? (See Lesson 5)
3. Could the behavior _____ [14] others or cause others to sin? (See Lesson 11)
4. Do I feel God is explicitly calling me to not do it? (See Lesson 11)

Lesson 9: Godliness (continued)

If you answer "Yes" to any of the questions, then you shouldn't do it. That doesn't necessarily mean it's sinful behavior nor one you should use to judge others, but it does mean that it's inappropriate for you.

What about times when I don't feel like being godly?

Godliness is not dependent on our emotions as if we need to wait until we feel like acting godly. It should be a natural result of the _____ [15] Christ has worked in us - a reflection of the prior disciplines of faith, moral excellence, knowledge, self-control, and patient endurance. Just as a husband should let his faithfulness to his wife be driven by his wedding vows and not whether he feels like being faithful or not, in the same way we need to demonstrate godliness due to our surrender and _____ [16] to Christ and not on whether we feel like being godly or not.

How did Jesus demonstrate godliness?

Jesus showed compassion to people in many ways. He never refused anyone who asked Him for help, but He also had compassion on and ministered to some who didn't ask Him. For example, he ministered to the Samaritan woman at the well (John 4:1-42), a lame man by the Pool of Bethesda (John 5:1-15), a man blind from birth (John 9:1-41), a widow's dead son (Luke 7:11-17), etc.

Read Mark 6:30-34. This is the introduction of when Jesus fed over five thousand people—the only miracle recorded in all four gospels. This miracle was at a time when Jesus didn't "feel" like being _____ [17]. That is, He and his disciples were grieving over the loss of John the Baptist, were hungry and tried to get away to rest. But when the people came, He had compassion on them and ministered powerfully to them.

How did other Christians in church history demonstrate godliness?

In Acts 3, Peter and John had compassion on and healed a lame man who only expected a handout. In Acts 10, God used Peter to open the gospel to the Gentiles even though Peter was resistant at first. He thought he was being godly by maintaining the Jewish customs like abstaining from certain foods (Acts 10:9-16) and not wanting to enter the home of Gentiles (Acts 10:28); this was a common view even among Jewish Christians (Acts 11:1-3). Even so, Peter honored God by following what He was leading him to do.

Despite this, Peter didn't always model godliness. Read Galatians 2:9-16. Although Peter was a "pillar of the church" and one of Jesus' closest friends, He struggled with _____ [18] as Paul described. From this we not only learn how godliness can be difficult for any Christian, but as we strive to become like Christ we also need brotherly kindness from other Christians to lovingly confront us about our sin.

In what ways have you struggled with godliness shown to others in need? Or at work? Or at church? Or with other behaviors considered forbidden by some Christians?

Read the book of 1 Corinthians once in the week – two chapters per day (or as a stretch goal read it two times). What parts stood out to you the most? What unique characteristics about Christ does Paul describe? In what ways does this book help you to become more like Christ?

[1] honor; [2] others; [3] compassion; [4] expects; [5] byproduct; [6] own world; [7] giving; [8] receiving; [9] surrender; [10] honor; [11] enthusiasm; [12] excellence; [13] forbid; [14] offend; [15] transformation; [16] commitment; [17] godly; [18] hypocrisy

Lesson 10: Brotherly Kindness

Lesson Summary
- Brotherly kindness is a way of honoring Christ by demonstrating love for other Christians.
- If our convictions about something differ from other Christians, then we can show brotherly kindness by not judging them and by not doing anything to offend them or cause them to stumble.
- One of the greatest ways to demonstrate brotherly kindness is through forgiveness; Jesus commands us to forgive others as an act of obedience to Him regardless of how we feel.

Bible Reading: *Hebrews*
- Minimum Homework: Read the entire book one time (2 chapters per day)
- Stretch Goal: Read the entire book two times (4 chapters per day)

Hymn: Remember Christ, Our Savior
(written by Robert E. Smith, 1990)

Remember Christ, our Savior Who paid the debts you owed,
To God the Heavenly Father and to you mercy showed.
When others sin against you be ready to forgive.
Since you have been forgiven with them in peace now live.

Go first to find your brother, your sister or your friend.
Do not reveal to others the hurt you need to mend.
Confront in humble spirit the one whose sin caused pain
That he might seek forgiveness and you a friend regain.

O Father, Son, and Spirit, O Patient Trinity,
Who lifts from us sin's burden and from its debt sets free.
Grant us the will to pardon all those who us offend
That we might enter heaven with them when ages end.

Lesson 10: Brotherly Kindness

Two kinds of love?
In the English language we have one word for love where we use the same word to say we love ice cream as we do to say we love our children. Obviously the type of love we imply is very different, but the New Testament (which was written in Greek) has several different ways to describe love.

The two most common words for love in the New Testament are phileo (fi-LAY-o) and agape (uh-GOP-ay). Phileo is the word we use to describe "_____[1] love" (or _____[1] kindness), while agape is generally interpreted as "unconditional love". Lesson 11 will go more in depth into describing the differences between them. For this lesson, we'll focus on brotherly kindness.

What is brotherly kindness?
It's generally referred to as a _____[2] kind of love. It's also interpreted as an admiration or affection that comes from inspiration. Since it's different from agape which means "unconditional love", then we can presume that phileo is a "conditional love".

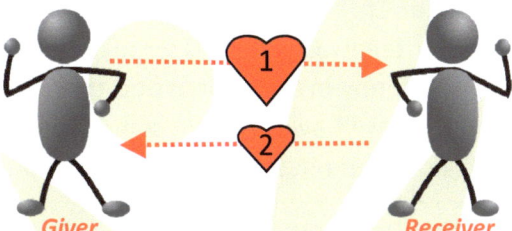

1. The Giver initiates love (agape) or brotherly kindness to the Receiver

2. The Receiver responds with brotherly kindness to the Giver (in gratitude)

Giver   Receiver

How is this brotherly kindness conditional? Generally the brotherly kindness shown is in response to receiving kindness or given due to a mutual expectation of receiving kindness in return. That is, as long as the Receiver continues to receive brotherly kindness from the Giver, then the Receiver will continue to _____[3] the brotherly kindness to the Giver as a sense of duty or gratitude. But if the Giver offends the Receiver or stops giving brotherly kindness, then the Receiver will probably stop returning it.

Brotherly kindness begins as a duty
Brotherly kindness is the natural next step from the prior external discipline of godliness. As we learned in Lesson 9, godliness is honoring Jesus in what we do. Brotherly kindness is honoring and serving our fellow Christians in what we do. Just as godliness is a duty that begins with a _____[4] to do what is right to honor Christ, brotherly kindness is a duty that begins with a _____[4] to do what is right to honor our fellow brothers and sisters in Christ. So honoring and serving fellow Christians is another way to honor Christ.

How do I demonstrate brotherly kindness to other Christians?
Read the entire chapter of Romans 14. In this passage, Paul gives very clear instructions on how we can demonstrate brotherly kindness to one another. He uses the subject of food to address the _____[5] between two types of Christians: those who are "weak in faith" (v. 1) and those who aren't. Today, we may substitute his subject of food with other issues in which Christians have varying convictions such as smoking, drinking, gambling, etc.

We can conclude from Paul's instructions that he isn't questioning IF the people with these convictions are in the faith, rather he's challenging the maturity of their faith. We can further

Lesson 10: Brotherly Kindness (continued)

conclude that despite the disagreement between Christians, the subject of food is not essential to Christianity and therefore not an issue that should cause _____ [6].

Paul expects those who are "weak in faith" to not judge others having fewer convictions. Despite this, he seems to have higher _____ [7] on those who are not "weak in faith" where he strongly instructs them to avoid what could offend or cause a fellow Christian to stumble.

Overall, there are three aspects for each type of Christian:
- **Conviction**: how firmly you believe in something.
- **Consideration**: how much _____ [8] you allow for someone who believes differently than you.
- **Contribution**: how much love you show through your words or actions despite your disagreement.

Convictions: Many (v. 2, 14, 23)
Consideration: Don't judge those who don't have same convictions (v. 3-4).
Contribution: Be faithful to your own convictions, but don't condemn others by them (v. 10-14, 23).

"Weak in faith"   Not "Weak in faith"

Convictions: Few or none (v. 22)
Consideration: Don't look down on those who have convictions (v. 3, 10).
Contribution: Avoid behavior that may offend a brother or cause them to stumble (v. 13-15, 20-22).

Paul isn't implying that the weaker Christian's conviction should also be considered sinful for everyone else, but acting on it and offending our fellow Christian is wrong and could tempt them to fall into what is sinful to them. If we are to "aim for harmony in the church and try to build each other up" (v. 19), then we need to not only give consideration to those having strong convictions, but we must _____ [9] brotherly kindness to them by not offending them with our actions.

> *What level of convictions do you have? How can you show consideration (tolerance) and contribute brotherly kindness to others who have different convictions?*

What do I do if I offend or am offended by another Christian?
Read Luke 17:1-10. On the surface, it appears this contains three different messages: 1) Forgiveness in v. 1-4; 2) Faith in v. 5-6; and 3) a parable in v. 7-10. However, this is actually one continuous message.

In v. 1-4, Jesus clearly talked about forgiveness. When Jesus gave the example of forgiving our brother seven times (or "seventy times seven" in Matthew 18:22), He was _____ [10] to make the point that we should not be counting how often our brother sins against us. The reason is that if we have truly forgiven him, then we should not be holding those prior offenses against him.

Due to Jesus' exaggeration, it seems unnatural to forgive someone who offends you so many times for the same thing. In fact, it would seem to require _____ [11] faith which is why the disciples ask Jesus to increase their faith. But Jesus used another exaggeration by describing how supernatural power (like uprooting a tree by your words) can be done by such a tiny amount of faith. It seems He exaggerated this to sarcastically imply that faith has nothing to do with forgiveness; it's not a supernatural feat.

Then Jesus' parable in Luke 17:7-10 just reinforces His point. A more modern application of this parable could be compared to eating in a formal restaurant. When the waiter comes to take your order, would you normally ask the waiter to sit down at your table and enjoy the meal with you? No, our expectation is that we are not concerned with how tired the waiter is, we expect our food to be ordered and delivered quickly. In this example, we are the waiter serving _____ [12] where His order in v.4 is "you must forgive". Therefore, we must obey His order as "unworthy servants who have simply done our duty" (v.10).

Lesson 10: Brotherly Kindness (continued)

How can Jesus reasonably expect us to always forgive?
Read Matthew 18:21-35. This parable is a parallel of Luke 17 and a great example of why God requires us to forgive. In this parable, we are the unforgiving debtor where our sin debt that God forgave is like a debt of hundreds of millions of dollars. In comparison, what the other debtor owed to us is equal to over $10,000 - far less money than what we owed, yet still a large sum even by our standards.

It seems Jesus is acknowledging the _____[13] we feel when someone offends us, but it is still far less than what we've been forgiven. If we truly understood that contrast, then it should be very easy for us to forgive others. Therefore, we should not let our forgiveness of others be driven by how we feel nor by the sincerity of the other person's apology, but it should be driven by obedience in humble response to the far greater forgiveness we received from God.

How did Jesus demonstrate brotherly kindness?
Jesus' entire life is an expression of more than just brotherly kindness, but a deep _____[14] love (discussed more in Lesson 11). But one of the more notable examples of brotherly kindness where he demonstrated forgiveness is in Luke 23:34 where in the midst of being unjustly crucified as a criminal He prayed for His accusers "Father, forgive them, for they don't know what they are doing."

How did other Christians in church history demonstrate brotherly kindness?
Paul practiced what he preached in Romans 14. Although Acts 15 describes how the Church agreed that circumcision was not a requirement for Gentiles, Acts 16:1-5 describes how Paul circumcised Timothy anyway. Since many Jews had strong convictions about circumcision, Paul did this as _____[15] for their convictions to ensure there is less hindrance to the gospel.

In the mid-1700's, George Whitefield and John Wesley were very influential preachers during America's first

J. Wesley

Great Awakening. Though they were both used mightily by God to lead many souls to Christ, they had a sharp theological disagreement that lasted their entire lives. Despite this, they looked beyond their theological convictions and showed brotherly kindness through _____[16] admiration. In fact, a well known story is told that after Whitefield's death, John Wesley was asked if he would see him in heaven due to their different theological opinions about heaven. To paraphrase his reply he said "No, I think he will be so close to the throne of glory that I won't even get a glimpse of him."

G. Whitefield

Is there anyone you have not forgiven yet? If so, how does it feel knowing that Jesus commands us to forgive out of obedience? How has your unforgiveness affected your spiritual growth?

Read the book of Hebrews once in the week – two chapters per day (or as a stretch goal read it two times). What parts stood out to you the most? What unique characteristics about Christ does the author describe? In what ways does this book help you to become more like Christ?

[1] brotherly; [2] mutual friendship; [3] loyally return; [4] decision; [5] convictions; [6] division; [7] expectations; [8] tolerance; [9] contribute; [10] exaggerating; [11] supernatural; [12] Jesus; [13] severe pain; [14] unconditional; [15] consideration; [16] mutual

Lesson 11: Love

Lesson Summary
- Agape love is characterized by self-sacrifice without any expectation of that love being returned. If we are offended by the response of the one we're showing love to, then chances are it wasn't agape love.
- Jesus exemplified agape love throughout His earthly ministry and ultimately by sacrificing Himself for us.
- Jesus measures the value of sacrificial love by comparing it with the giver, not the receiver. That is, He is more concerned about our degree of sacrifice than the need of the one benefiting from the sacrifice.

 **Bible Reading:** *1 John*
- Minimum Homework: Read the entire book two times (2 chapters per day)
- Stretch Goal: Read the entire book four times (4 chapters per day)

 **Hymn: When I Survey the Wondrous Cross**
(written by Isaac Watts, 1707)

When I survey the wondrous cross on which the Prince of glory died,
My riches gain I count but loss, and pour contempt on all my pride.

Forbid it, Lord, that I should boast, save in the death of Christ my God!
All the vain things that charm me most, I sacrifice them to His blood.

See from His head, His hands, His feet, sorrow and love flow mingled down!
Die e'er such love and sorrow meet, or thorns compose so rich a crown?

His dying crimson, like a robe, spreads o'er His body on the tree;
Then I am dead to all the globe, and all the globe is dead to me.

Were the whole realm of nature mine, that were a present far too small;
Love so amazing, so divine, demands my soul, my life, my all.

Lesson 11: Love

What is (unconditional) love?

In Lesson 10 we learned the Bible refers to more than one type of love: phileo (brotherly kindness) and agape (unconditional love). Phileo love is generally what someone gives as a _____[1] to the love or affection it receives. It's conditional because the phileo love will continue to be shown as long as it continues to receive love (either agape or phileo).

Agape love is different because it is _____[2] whether or not the love is returned. It is a love that leads to action that often had originated outside of the very person giving it. For example, it's generally each mother's nature to initiate unconditional love for her child and demonstrate it by caring for the health, safety and needs of her child even though the child doesn't return that love in the same way. The child will tend to respond by returning a phileo, _____[3] love until he or she matures to respond with unconditional love.

1. The Giver initiates love (agape) to the Receiver and doesn't require their love to be returned.

2. The Receiver **may** respond with phileo or agape love to the Giver, but it isn't required.

Peter's view of these two types of love

Peter is the one who wrote the eight disciplines toward becoming like Christ (2 Peter 1:5-7) on which this discipleship guide is based. John 21:15-19 is a conversation that he and Jesus had that reveals how well Peter knows the difference between these two types of love. Below is an outline of their discussion with the different forms of love noted:

Jesus' Question	Peter's Answer	Jesus' Reply
1. Do you love (agape) me?	Yes, you know I love (phileo) You	Feed my lambs
2. Do you love (agape) me?	Yes, you know I love (phileo) You	Take care of my sheep
3. Do you love (phileo) me?	[Disturbed that Jesus questioned his phileo love]: You know everything. You know I love (phileo) You	Feed my sheep; Follow Me

When considering how these different Greek words for love were used, it seems Jesus is trying to ask Peter if he loves Him unconditionally, but Peter is only willing to admit to a conditional, _____[4] love. But when Jesus questions if Peter even has that devotional kind of love, Peter is grieved yet reassures Him that he does have that kind of love for Him. We don't exactly know what Peter was thinking, but we can speculate that his faith was being shaken (Luke 22:31-32). He just denied knowing the very Man to whom he devoted three years of his life. He may have felt confused yet resolute in following Christ just as in John 6:66-69 when he affirmed his allegiance to Christ after many other disciples left. Although that kind of devotion is admirable, Jesus is calling Peter to a deeper, _____[5] commitment.

Agape love always leads to self-sacrifice

Agape love never resides exclusively in our emotions. It becomes a part of our nature—who we are—which may be connected to our emotions, but is always _____[6] by self-sacrifice. Just as the agape love of a mother leads her to protect and care for her child, each of Jesus' replies to Peter in John 21 are a call to self-sacrifice, i.e., to give of himself to feed and care for the Church. Moreover, in v. 18—19 Jesus is calling Peter to the ultimate

Lesson 11: Love (continued)

demonstration of unconditional love, which is sacrificing _____[7] in the same way Jesus just had. Below are examples from scripture of agape love and the self-sacrifice that demonstrates it:

Scripture Reference	Who showed love?	What was the act of sacrifice?
John 3:16	God	Gave only begotten Son
Rom 5:8; Eph 2:4-5	God	Sent Christ while we were _____[8]
1 John 4:9-10	God	Sent Jesus to give us eternal life
John 3:35	Father	Put all things into Jesus' hands
John 14:21, 23	Jesus/Father	Reveals Himself; makes His home in us
2 Thes 2:16	Jesus/Father	Gave us eternal life and wonderful hope
Gal 2:20	Jesus	Gave _____[9] for me
2 Cor 12:14-15	Paul	Gave himself
John 13:34, 14:15, 14:24, 15:10, 15:12, 15:17	Christians	Love is given as a command for Christians to obey

How can I tell if the love I show is agape love?

A way to test if your love is unconditional like agape love is to ask yourself "Am I _____[10] by the response to my love?" A mother showing unconditional love to her baby doesn't expect the baby to return the love and therefore would not normally be offended when that love isn't returned. But when you try to show love to someone who ignores or rejects it, do you feel resentful or bitter? Do you secretly try to get even with them (using passive-aggression)? If so, then chances are it was not agape love.

Despite this, there is a difference between being offended by someone's response and being disappointed by their response. God had often expressed His anger and disappointment in Israel to whom He continually demonstrated His unconditional love (Matt 23:37). Just as a parent of a rebellious child may not expect their love to be returned, they may have a reasonable expectation of receiving respect and obedience. God is not very different where His love is not dependent on nor motivated by our respect and obedience. But if we say we love Him in return, then it should be reflected in our _____[11] to Him.

 Think of a time you did something out of love but were ignored or rejected by it. How did it make you feel? What response did you expect? What does this reveal about the type of love you showed?

How did Jesus demonstrate agape love?

Jesus is our perfect model for agape love who demonstrated this unconditional love throughout His life:
- **Birth**: Though Jesus was always God (John 1:1-4; Col 1:15-17), He gave up His divine privileges to become a _____[12] like us (Phil 2:6-8; 2 Cor 8:9; Heb 2:14-18, 10:4-5).
- **Earthly Ministry**: He was a humble servant (Phil 2:6-8; John 13:1-17) who sought only to please His Father (John 8:28-29) and taught the people about the Kingdom of heaven (Matt 13:24-52). He confirmed His teachings through many miraculous signs and wonders (Matt 11:3-4; John 2:23, 6:2, 7:31; Heb 2:3-4).
- **Death**: Even though He never sinned (2 Cor 5:21), He _____[13] (John 10:17-18; Isa 53:7) offered Himself as a sacrifice for our sin by taking the judgment and punishment we deserve (John 3:16-17; Rom 5:6-8; Gal 2:20; 1 John 4:9-10).
- **Resurrection**: When we trust in Christ for salvation, God declares us _____[14] (1 Pet 1:2; Rom 8:29-30; 2 Thes 2:13) and deposits His Holy Spirit in us—the same Spirit who raised Jesus from the dead and is our guarantee (Eph 1:13-14) and hope for our own resurrection (Eph 2:4-7; 2 Cor 5:14-17).

Lesson 11: Love (continued)

How did other Christians in church history demonstrate agape love?

There are three unique examples of people during the time of Christ who demonstrated unconditional love. Please read these stories and refer to the chart below that outlines the characteristics of each:

Question	Good Samaritan	Anointing Oil from Mary	Widow's Mite
Scripture reference	Luke 10:25-37	John 12:1-8	Luke 21:1-4
Who was the Giver?	A Samaritan man	Mary	Widow
What was the gift the Giver had sacrificed?	Time and money to care for the wounded man's life	Rare perfume valued at one year's wages ($35,000+)	Money that was a high percentage of what little she had
Who was the Receiver?	A wounded Jewish man	Jesus	The Temple (or church)
Did the Receiver ask for a gift?	No	No	Uncertain, but probably
Response from others	Probably thought nothing good comes from Samaritans	Disciples considered it a waste; could've been sold	Considered to be a very insignificant amount
Response from Jesus	Samaritan acted neighborly	Welcomed her gift; she'll be memorialized	Jesus said value was greater than what the rich gave

Based on these examples of self-sacrificing love, we can make the following conclusions:
- We often measure the value of a sacrifice by comparing the GIFT with the RECEIVER.
  - The lawyer who asked Jesus "who is my neighbor" was trying to determine who was worthy to be a receiver of the unconditional love he's required to give.
  - The disciples compared the value of the gift (a year's wages) to be far _____ [15] than the value of Jesus. They thought the poor (who they didn't know) are more worthy of the gift than Jesus.
- Jesus measures the value of a sacrifice by comparing the GIFT with the GIVER.
  - Jesus isn't concerned with who is receiving the gift as much as who is _____ [16] the gift and the amount of sacrifice that gift represents for the giver.
  - It seems Jesus expects us to make the sacrifice "local". That is, give to the need He sets before us (like a wounded person, local church, etc.) rather than a long-distance need (the poor—John 12:8).

Imagine you had $10,000 to donate to either your church's building repair or disaster victims in another country. The disaster victims may seem like a greater need, but Jesus is more concerned about our sacrifice than the one receiving our gift. Likewise, we shouldn't choose based on the need of the receiver, but on the need God has set immediately before us. Like the disciples, we may think that some donations are a "waste", but Jesus is far more concerned about our _____ [17] than the one receiving it.

In what ways do you think God is calling you to show unconditional love through sacrifice? What do you think is holding you back from making that sacrifice?

Read the book of 1 John twice in the week – two chapters per day (or as a stretch goal read it four times). What parts stood out to you the most? What unique characteristics about Christ does John describe? In what ways does this book help you to become more like Christ?

[1] response; [2] initiated; [3] conditional; [4] devotional; [5] self-sacrificing; [6] demonstrated; [7] his life; [8] sinners; [9] Himself; [10] offended; [11] obedience; [12] human being; [13] willingly; [14] righteous; [15] greater; [16] giving; [17] sacrifice

Lesson 12: Interpreting the Bible

Lesson Summary
- Some misinterpretations of scripture have challenged many uninformed Christians to the point of
- abandoning their faith. It's critical that we understand scripture to avoid any counterfeit teaching.
- The essential elements of saving faith (e.g., judgment, atonement and resurrection) remain universal and timeless. We must beware of tabloid and folk theologies that may divert us from the essentials.
- A three step method for interpreting and applying scripture is asking 1) What did it mean when it was written?, 2) What is the universal principle?, and 3) How do I apply it to my life today?

Bible Reading: *The entire New Testament*
Develop a daily plan for reading the Bible consistently, starting with 2 to 3 chapters a day in the New Testament. With a stretch goal of 5 chapters a day, you can finish it every 2 months.

The Nicene Creed
(written at the First Church Council of Nicaea, 325)

We believe in one God the Father Almighty, Maker of heaven and earth, and of all things visible and invisible.

And in one Lord Jesus Christ, the only-begotten Son of God, begotten of the Father before all worlds, God of God, Light of Light, Very God of Very God, begotten, not made, being of one substance with the Father by whom all things were made; who for us men, and for our salvation, came down from heaven, and was incarnate by the Holy Spirit of the Virgin Mary, and was made man, and was crucified also for us under Pontius Pilate. He suffered and was buried, and the third day he rose again according to the Scriptures, and ascended into heaven, and sits on the right hand of the Father. And he shall come again with glory to judge both the quick and the dead, whose kingdom shall have no end.

And we believe in the Holy Spirit, the Lord and Giver of Life, who proceeds from the Father and the Son, who with the Father and the Son together is worshipped and glorified, who spoke by the prophets.

And we believe one holy catholic and apostolic Church. We acknowledge one baptism for the remission of sins. And we look for the resurrection of the dead, and the life of the world to come. Amen.

Lesson 12: Interpreting the Bible

A brief recap
The prior eleven lessons are based on 2 Peter 1:3-11 and outline the eight disciplines in v. 5-7 in more detail. Peter states in v. 4 that God _____ [1] we can "share His divine nature" - our ultimate goal of becoming like Christ. This is done when we "make every effort to respond to God's promises" (v. 5) by working hard (v. 10) to grow in these disciplines (v. 8).

Why do I need to learn how to interpret the Bible?
Have you ever wondered why so many Christians "fall away" (v. 10), or can't "escape the world's corruption caused by human desires" (v. 4), or become "shortsighted or blind, forgetting that they have been cleaned from their old sins" (v. 9)? Is God powerless (v. 3) or unfaithful (v. 4)?

If we trust in God's power and faithfulness, then we can only conclude these Christians didn't "make every effort" (v. 5) to follow these disciplines. Why weren't they faithful to follow the disciplines? It very often can be linked to misinterpreting scripture that challenged their faith. The more _____ [2] we are at interpreting the Bible accurately, then the more confident and grounded we can become in our faith to keep us from abandoning it.

The Bible says "There is no God"
It's true! It can be found in Psalm 14:1 and Psalm 53:1. In fact it actually says "Only fools say in their hearts, 'There is no God.'" This passage was purposely quoted out of _____ [3] to make a point. When you first read that title, did it seem obvious to you that it was taken out of context? If so, why? Is it because it is an obvious contradiction to our faith? It certainly is!

For example, examine the three $100 bills below. Which one is real?

The first one is obviously not real. It is so different from what you know and expect to be the real $100 bill that it's immediately apparent. However, the next two may not be so obvious. They are very similar, but actually the one on the far right is counterfeit containing 7 very subtle mistakes. This is not as apparent because it is so similar in design to the real $100 bill.

In the same way, some things we hear about God are obviously wrong because they contradict what we know to be _____ [4] to our faith. But often there are other beliefs that misrepresent God and our faith that aren't as obvious to us. There are even lots of passages from scripture that many well-meaning Christians take out of context. Some of it is harmless, but some can be very harmful if we misinterpret scripture and misapply it to our lives.

Testing for counterfeits
The best way to detect counterfeit money is to study real money closely so that the counterfeits appear obvious. In the same way, it is critical that we grow in our faith and understand the scriptures so we can accurately _____ [5] and _____ [6] the truth (2 Tim 2:15).

Read Acts 17:11-12. The Bereans eagerly listened to Paul and Silas but they didn't blindly accept it. Instead they diligently researched it in scripture to validate what they told them and concluded that Paul and Silas were right. As a result, it led to a great revival in the city.

Lesson 12: Interpreting the Bible (continued)

Just like the Bereans, we need to be diligent to test with scripture what we hear others teach about God. But is it reasonable to test everything we hear? Not necessarily. At a minimum we should test what is essential to our saving faith which is the foundation for the disciplines of becoming like Christ.

With so many church doctrines, how can I know which are essential for saving faith?

If salvation is available to everyone for all time (John 3:16; Matt 28:19; Acts 1:8), then for certain beliefs or doctrines to be considered essential for salvation, these essentials must also be:
- *Historically Timeless*: they must apply the same _____ [7] as at the time of Christ.
- *Culturally Boundless*: they must apply the same for all _____ [8] in any location or culture.
- *Uniquely Accessible*: since salvation isn't "automatic", they must be specific (not abstract) and attainable.

Church doctrine has significantly evolved over the last few thousand years. Over time we have come to a better and more accurate understanding of scripture and formalized that understanding into various doctrines, such as the trinity, the rapture, the infallibility of scripture, and even the atonement.

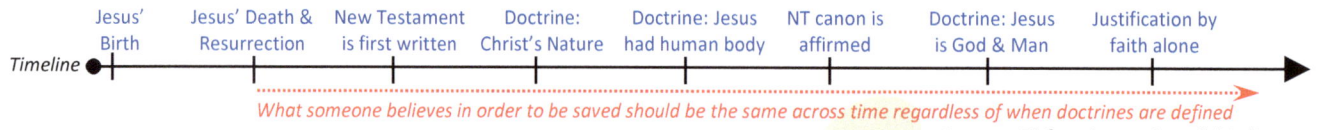

What someone believes in order to be saved should be the same across time regardless of when doctrines are defined

See page 70 for a larger view of this diagram

If salvation is "historically timeless", then what a person in 200 A.D. believed in order to be saved did not necessarily include the doctrines defined after 200 A.D. In other words, a person could've been saved in 200 A.D. and possibly had beliefs that _____ [9] today's church doctrines.

What are the essentials of saving faith?

Salvation begins at the point of justification. Lessons 1—4 explain this and lay the foundation for faith which is simply made up of judgment, atonement, and resurrection. Anything else may arguably be non-essential if they don't qualify as historically timeless, culturally boundless, and uniquely accessible. Despite this, there are many other beliefs that support our faith and are critical for _____ [10] as we grow to become like Christ, but that doesn't mean they're essential for salvation.

For example, a woman's fertilized egg may define someone as "human", but in order to sustain that life after fertilization, it's critical that the baby receives nourishment. In the same way, we need to distinguish what gets us *born* into salvation (justification) and what *nourishes* us in salvation (sanctification). This distinction is critical because if someone challenges a belief that is essential to saving faith, we need to have no _____ [11] for anything that contradicts it. Similarly, if someone challenges a belief that is not essential for salvation, then we can have more tolerance and debate it freely.

Beware of Tabloid and Folk Theology

Theology is basically what you believe about God. It's not just for Bible scholars. Everyone has a unique theology that is about as different as our own experiences in life. As you continue in your Christian journey, it is critical that you understand what you believe so you can identify and avoid two types of theology:
- *Tabloid Theology*: A belief based on a sensationalized story or experience such as people claiming they were visited by angels. Even if these stories were true, they shouldn't divert us from our essential faith.
- *Folk Theology*: A belief based on what we always believed. For example, enforcing personal hygiene on others because "cleanliness is next to godliness". Despite the practical wisdom, it is not based on scripture and such beliefs should not _____ [12] us from our essential faith.

The Bible is literature

The Bible is a collection of 66 books that were written over 1500 years by more than 50 different authors

Lesson 12: Interpreting the Bible (continued)

using 3 different languages. It is literature because it includes many literary styles such as poetry, proverbs, _____ [13] descriptions, prophecy and personal letters, and it includes many literary devices such as riddles, laws, hyperbole, parables, imagery, lyrics, etc.

When you hear someone say "Once upon a time…" you know immediately they're about to tell you a fairy tale. In the same way, the Bible has many idioms that were understood by its intended audience. Most of the Bible was written to specific people in a specific time with a specific message for a specific purpose. Therefore, we cannot use the Bible like an dictionary as if each part stands on its own. It needs to be understood in context of the immediate passage, book, and _____ [14] of the rest of the Bible.

How do we interpret the Bible in the right context?

Don't just ask "what does that scripture mean *to me*?". But instead we should ask "What does that scripture mean?" We should understand the original _____ [15] of the scripture to see how God intends for us to apply it to our lives. Here is a three step method for interpreting a scripture in the right context:

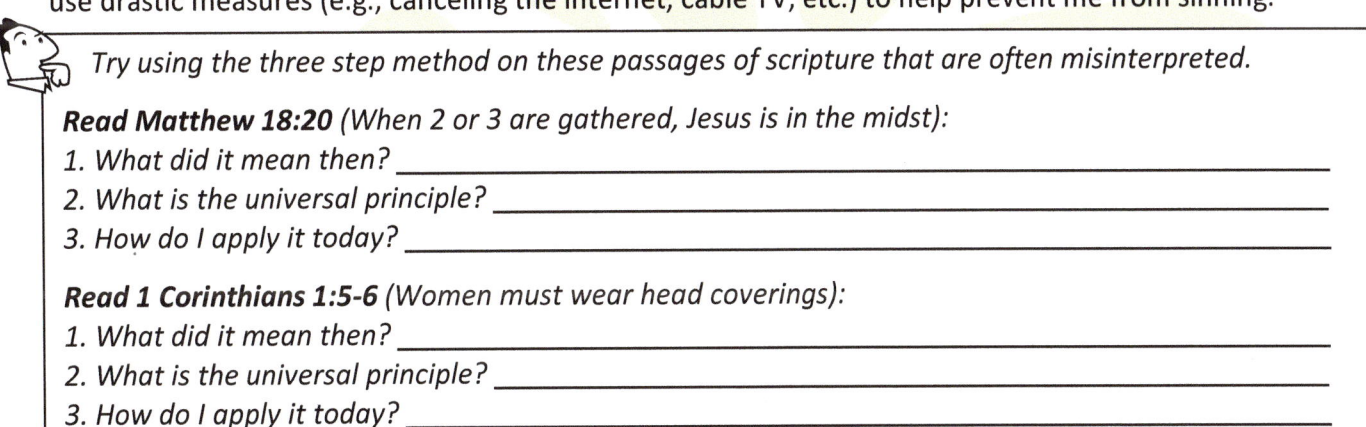

1 What did the scripture mean at the time it was written?
- Who's the author & their intent? Who's their audience?
- What literary style/device is used?
- What are the historical events and culture at that time?
- How does it fit with surrounding verses, chapters, etc.?

2 What is the universal principle from that scripture?

3 How do I apply that universal principle to my life today?
- What is the overall principle God is intending to say?
- Is that principle consistent with the essentials for faith?
- Is that principle contradicted anywhere else in the Bible?

See page 71 for a larger view of this diagram

For example, read Matthew 5:29-30. Here's how the three step method is used to interpret this passage:
1. What did it mean then? It appears Jesus didn't intend that we literally pluck out our eyes, but used a hyperbole to emphasize His point. He said this right after saying in v. 28 how lust is like adultery.
2. What is the universal principle? We should use drastic measures to prevent ourselves from sinning.
3. How do I apply it today? If what I see is tempting me to sin (e.g., internet, cable TV, etc.), then I should use drastic measures (e.g., canceling the internet, cable TV, etc.) to help prevent me from sinning.

Try using the three step method on these passages of scripture that are often misinterpreted.

Read Matthew 18:20 *(When 2 or 3 are gathered, Jesus is in the midst):*
1. What did it mean then? _____
2. What is the universal principle? _____
3. How do I apply it today? _____

Read 1 Corinthians 1:5-6 *(Women must wear head coverings):*
1. What did it mean then? _____
2. What is the universal principle? _____
3. How do I apply it today? _____

 Develop a plan for reading the Bible consistently. For example, try reading 2 to 3 chapters a day in the New Testament. If you read 5 chapters a day, you'd have the entire New Testament finished in just 2 months. If you repeat this, that means you could read it 6 times a year!

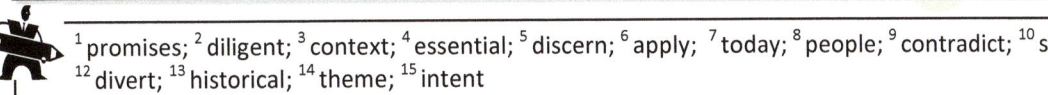

[1] promises; [2] diligent; [3] context; [4] essential; [5] discern; [6] apply; [7] today; [8] people; [9] contradict; [10] sanctification; [11] tolerance; [12] divert; [13] historical; [14] theme; [15] intent

Index of Scripture References

Deuteronomy

6:5	25

Psalm

14:1	53
19	14
53:1	53

Isaiah

53:6	18
53:7	18, 50

Matthew

4	35
4:1-11	35, 39
5:21-22	15, 26
5:27-28	15, 26
5:29-30	33, 55
6:1-4	35
6:16-18	34
6:19-24	35
8:23-27	39
11:3-4	50
11:10	31
12:3-8	31
12:22-37	39
12:34-35	34
13:20-21	37
13:24-52	50
15:18-19	34
18:20	55
18:21-35	48
18:22	47
22:36-46	31
21:44	19
23:23	31
23:37	50
25:31-46	41
26:36-44	35
28:19	54

Mark

1:22	31
6:30-34	43
12:10-11	31
12:29-30	25

Luke

4:16-30	39
4:17-22	31
7:11-16	21, 43
10:25-37	41, 51
13:1-4	38
17	48
17:1-10	47
20:1-8	39
20:20-40	39
21:1-4	51
22:3-6	39
22:31-32	49
22:54-65	39
23:34	48
24:44-47	31

John

1:1-2	30
1:1-4	50
2:23	50
3:16-17	50, 54
3:18	15
3:35	50
3:36	15
4:1-42	43
5:1-15	43
6:2	50
6:45	30
6:66-69	49
7:1-9	39
7:21-38	31
7:31	50
8:17	31
8:28-29	50
9	43
9:1-3	38
10:17-18	18, 50
10:34-35	31
11:1-45	21
12:1-8	51
13:1-17	50
13:18	31

John (cont'd)

13:34	50
14:6	9
14:15	50
14:21-24	50
15:10	50
15:12	50
15:17	50
17:12	31
21	49
21:15-19	49

Acts

1:8	54
2:16-35	31
3	43
3:22-26	31
4:1-22	39
4:11-26	31
5:17-42	39
6	31
7	31
7:60-8:3	39
9:1-2	39
9:3-19	39
9:23-25	39
10	43
11:1-3	43
12:1-5	39
13:50-14:7	39
14:19-20	39
15	48
16:1-5	48
16:22-34	39
17:11-12	53
21:26-36	39
23:12-31	39
27	39

Romans

1:17	31
1:18-19	18
1:20	14

Romans (cont'd)

1:24	18
1:32	18
2:14-15	14
2:17-20	14
3:19-20	14
3:21-22	14
3:9	14
3:9-10	17
3:19	17
3:23	17
5:3-4	37
5:6-8	18, 50
5:8	50
6:6-7	27
6:12-13	27
8	21
8:12	22
8:14-16	9
8:29-30	22, 50
8:31-39	23
12:2	26
14	48

1 Corinthians

1:5-6	55
2:11-12	29
15:16-17	21

2 Corinthians

4:7-17	39
5:14-17	50
5:17	25
5:21	18, 26, 50
6:3-10	39
8:9	50
11:18-12:10	39
12:14-15	50
13:5	34

Galatians

2:9-16	43
2:20	25, 50
5:22-23	37

Index of Scripture References (continued)

Ephesians

1:13-14	22, 50
1:16-18	29
2:4-7	50
4:21-24	27, 34
6:5-9	42

Philippians

1:29	37
2:10-11	19
2:13	10
2:6-8	50
4:8	27

Colossians

1:9-10	29
1:15-17	50
1:28	5
3:1-3	27, 34
3:10	27

2 Thessalonians

2:13	50
2:16	50

1 Timothy

3:2	35
3:11	35

2 Timothy

2:15	53
3:15-17	30

Hebrews

1:1-2	30
2:3-4	50
2:14	17
2:14-18	50
4:12-13	26
4:15	18, 26, 35
6:17-19	22
6:18-19	37
10:4-5	18, 50
10:19-23	22
11	13

James

1:2-4	37
2:10	15

James *(cont'd)*

2:14	13
2:21-22	13
2:24	13
2:14-26	23

1 Peter

1:2	50
1:13-16	35
2:18-19	42

2 Peter

1:3—11	5, 8, 10, 53
1:5-7	49
3:15-17	30

1 John

4:9-10	50

Index and Glossary by Subject

The definitions below are primarily in context of their usage within this Discipleship Guide.

Subject	Page #
Adoption	8-11, 14, 20-22, 25

It is when we become adopted into God's family through the process of salvation. It implies that we were formerly not a part of His family but He made a way to graft us into His family.
See also "Redemption" and "Salvation".

Subject	Page #
Adversity	36-41

See "Suffering".

| **Agape** | 45, 48-51 |

One of four common Greek words for love. Unlike phileo love, it implies an unconditional love that is self-sacrificing and doesn't require the acts of love that are shown to be mutual or returned.
See also "Love".

| **Assurance** | 13, 23, 36, 37 |

Having an unwavering confidence in how God views you. For salvation, it's boldly and confidently knowing that God has justified and placed in right-standing (righteousness) those He has adopted into His family (Christians).

| **Atonement** | 11, 15-18, 21, 23, 26, 39, 52, 54 |

The second of three essential parts of saving faith. It means to restore what was lost or broken, or to reconcile or repay a debt. The death of Christ is the act of atonement where He paid the punishment we deserve and therefore has made a way to restore our broken and severed relationship with God caused by our sin.
See also "Resurrection".

| **Born Again** | 9-10 |

The term depicting the spiritual rebirth a Christian experiences at the point of justification. It is when we allow our old lives to spiritually die and be reborn to a new life of being adopted into God's family.
See also "Christian" and "Salvation".

| **Brotherly Kindness** | 11, 37, 42-47, 49 |

The seventh of eight disciplines outlined in 2 Peter 1:5-7. It is demonstrated by working to not offend other Christians and pursuing forgiveness.
See also "Phileo", "Love" and "External Disciplines".

| **Christian** | 8-11, 14, 17, 20-23, 25-26, 37-38, 41-46, 53 |

Literally, someone who is like or a follower of Christ. It also refers to someone who is saved, justified, born again, and adopted into God's family.
See also "Born Again" and "Saved".

| **Church** | 5, 31, 35, 39-40, 42-43, 46-47, 49, 52, 54 |

Universally, it's the collective body of Christians worldwide and for all time. Locally, it's a subset of Christians who are generally like-minded in their doctrine (especially non-essentials) and gather regularly to worship, fellowship, serve, and grow in their faith.

| **Commandments** | 12, 14 |

Any direct command by God especially as recorded in the Bible. It specifically includes the ten commandments as well as any commands Jesus has given (e.g., forgiveness, love one another, obedience, etc.).
See also "Revelation".

| **Condemnation** | 10, 14-15, 21 |

The first of four stages in a Christian's life and the only stage of life for non-Christians. It's the stage of being under God's judgment due to the sins we've committed. It's similar to a criminal having a warrant out for his arrest due to the overwhelming evidence of his guilt; when he's caught, he will face judgment and sentencing. In the same way, our sin is the evidence of our guilt and once we're "caught" via death, we will face God at judgment.
See also "Judgment" and "Justification".

| **Conscience** | 12, 14, 19, 22 |

The God-imparted "inner voice" that generally reflects God's moral standards (formally codified as the ten commandments). Everyone has a conscience, though the degree to which we're sensitive to our conscience varies greatly.
See also "Revelation".

| **Consideration** | 46-47 |

Giving favor to someone else or being considerate of them. Specifically, it implies the amount of tolerance we may allow for someone else who has different beliefs from us.

| **Context** | 30, 37, 53, 55 |

The original and intended meaning of a passage of scripture. Understanding this is critical before attempting to extract and apply the universal principle from that scripture.
See also "Scripture".

| **Contribution** | 46 |

Imparting an act or expression of love. Specifically, it implies the acts or words of love we may give for someone else who has different beliefs from us.

| **Conviction** | 14, 44-47 |

For the purpose of this guide, it refers to a firm belief and how strongly you believe in it, such as in the essentials of faith versus a non-essential issue.

Index and Glossary by Subject (continued)

The definitions below are primarily in context of their usage within this Discipleship Guide.

Subject	Page #
Creation	12, 14, 19, 26

Everything created by our Creator, from everything in or on the earth to everything in the universe.
See also "Revelation".

Subject	Page #
Disciple	5, 7, 43, 46, 49, 51

Someone who follows or learns from someone else. For the purpose of this guide, it's a follower of Christ or even someone who is learning from someone else on how to follow Christ.
See also "Christian" and "Born Again".

Subject	Page #
Discipleship	5, 7

The process or method a disciple uses to follow Christ.

Subject	Page #
Doctrine	31, 52, 54

A belief or principle that is formally recognized or approved by an authorizing body (like church or government). For Christianity, it's a belief that has been communicated by Church leadership (i.e., God or Christ Himself or through His messengers like the apostles, prophets, etc.), tested and validated with scripture, and formally defined and generally accepted and taught throughout Church history. Every essential of the faith is doctrine, but not every doctrine is an essential of the faith.
See also "Essentials of Faith".

Subject	Page #
Essentials Of Faith	7, 11, 46, 52-55

A belief that is critically required for salvation. "sine qua non" (SIN-a kwah NON) is Latin for "without which not"; this phrase implies an indispensible condition that without a particular belief, then salvation would not be possible. The essentials of faith will always be historically timeless, culturally boundless, and uniquely accessible. We should have little tolerance for any belief that contradicts the essentials of faith, yet show love and compassion for anyone holding those contradicting beliefs so that we can communicate the essentials for salvation to them.
See also "Doctrine".

Subject	Page #
External Disciplines	11, 25, 37, 41-42, 45

The last four of eight disciplines outlined in 2 Peter 1:5-7 that are described as necessary for growing in faith and becoming like Christ. These disciplines are patient endurance, godliness, brotherly kindness, and love. As external disciplines, they are built on the foundation of the four internal disciplines and are generally more visible by others.
See also "Internal Disciplines".

Subject	Page #
Faith	10-14, 16, 21-23, 25, 28-31, 33-34, 36-38, 43, 45-46, 49, 52-55

The first of eight disciplines outlined in 2 Peter 1:5-7. It is the primary discipline upon which the other eight disciplines founded. Without faith, salvation isn't possible no matter how faithful someone is to the other seven disciplines; therefore, faith is considered essential for salvation. Faith is centered on the biblical beliefs of judgment, atonement, and resurrection.
See also "Moral Excellence" and "Internal Disciplines".

Subject	Page #
Fasting	32, 34

A personal discipline that is encouraged but not required in scripture; it is demonstrated by withholding something that is otherwise desirable and biblically permissible such as food. In this discipleship guide, it is a secondary discipline for self control that helps filter what comes INTO us.
See also "Self-Control".

Subject	Page #
Folk Theology	52, 54

A spiritual belief that is based on what was always believed and accepted as truth yet is neither a church doctrine nor clearly grounded in scripture. It is generally characterized by a belief based on what seems logical or has commonly been taught, but has no or very weak biblical support (e.g., "cleanliness is next to godliness", or abstinence from dancing, smoking, eating meat, circumcision, etc.). There may be nothing inherently wrong with these, but they should not influence our essential beliefs especially if they contradict any part of scripture.
See also "Tabloid Theology", "Doctrine", and "Non-Essentials of Faith".

Subject	Page #
Forgiveness	15, 18, 25, 33, 44, 46-47

Not holding against someone else the pain or offense they inflicted on us. Jesus is our perfect model of forgiveness who not only forgave us for our sins committed against Him, but made a way of salvation for us through the atonement and resurrection. He also commands (not suggests) that we forgive one another as a demonstration of brotherly kindness and love.
See also "Brotherly Kindness".

Subject	Page #
Giving	32, 35, 41, 45, 49, 51

A personal discipline demonstrated by expending some part of us (money, time, etc.) for the sake of the Lord in a way that we consider valuable. In this discipleship guide, it is a secondary discipline for self control that helps filter what goes OUT from us.
See also "Self-Control".

Index and Glossary by Subject (continued)

The definitions below are primarily in context of their usage within this Discipleship Guide.

Subject	Page #

Glorification — 10
The last of four stages in a Christian's life. It's the stage that Christians are promised to reach after death when we finally step into the glorious presence of God. It is in this stage in the future that we look forward to when we will be saved and free from the presence of sin.
See also "Condemnation".

Godliness — 11, 26, 37, 40-43, 45, 54
The sixth of eight disciplines outlined in 2 Peter 1:5-7. It is demonstrated by asking "what would honor Jesus?" and acting on it. It is seen in how we support others who are facing adversity and how we behave at work to our leadership and subordinates. It is not dependent on how we feel (our emotions) nor whether we think others will see our behavior.
See also "Brotherly Kindness" and "External Disciplines".

Internal Disciplines — 11, 24-25, 27, 33-34, 37
The first four of eight disciplines outlined in 2 Peter 1:5-7 that are described as necessary for growing in faith and becoming like Christ. These disciplines are faith, moral excellence, knowledge, and self control. As internal disciplines, they serve as the foundation for the four external disciplines and are generally not as visible or measurable by others.
See also "External Disciplines".

Judgment — 11, 15, 19, 50, 52, 54
The first of three essential parts of saving faith that shows how we are condemned by God because of our sin. It begins with recognizing that no person is "good", but we have all fallen short of God's moral standards as He has revealed through His ten commandments and confirmed in each person's conscience. This shortfall is our sin for which God said we are all guilty and condemned to eternal separation from Him in Hell.
See also "Condemnation" and "Atonement".

Justification — 10, 14, 22, 31, 54
The second of four stages in a Christian's life. It's the stage that represents a moment in time when a person becomes a Christian and is adopted into God's family. This moment of salvation occurs when an unbeliever is broken before God, repents for their sin that separated them from God and trusts in Christ as their only source for salvation. It is at this stage in the past for Christians when we were saved and became free from the penalty of sin.
See also "Sanctification", "Redemption" and "Salvation".

Knowledge — 10-11, 25, 27-31, 33-34, 37, 43
The third of eight disciplines outlined in 2 Peter 1:5-7. God is our primary source for spiritual knowledge; He wants us to seek and learn from Him to help us grow to become like Christ. One of the most effective ways to do this is through regularly reading and applying the Bible to our lives.
See also "Self-Control" and "Internal Disciplines".

Love — 11, 14-15, 28, 30, 37, 44-51
The last of eight disciplines outlined in 2 Peter 1:5-7. It is the pinnacle of our discipleship toward becoming like Christ where we are most like Him and most likely to reflect Him to the lost when we demonstrate self-sacrificing love to one another.
See also "Agape", "Faith" and "External Disciplines".

Moral Excellence — 11, 24-26, 33-34, 37, 43
The second of eight disciplines outlined in 2 Peter 1:5-7. It's begins with a desire to turn from sin and not re-build the very walls that once separated us from God that we had just repented of. As such, it's characterized by allowing God to transform our heart and mind so that we wouldn't even desire the very things that tempt and lead us into sin.
See also "Knowledge" and "Internal Disciplines".

Non-Essentials Of Faith — 7, 11, 46, 52-55
Any belief that is not critically required (or essential) for salvation. The non-essentials of faith will not be either historically timeless, culturally boundless, or uniquely accessible. We should have high tolerance for any belief that doesn't contradict the essentials of faith, and only debate those beliefs among Christians with a non-divisive attitude of love and humility.
See also "Folk Theology", "Tabloid Theology" and "Essentials of Faith".

Offense — 46
To feel emotionally inflicted by the words or actions of someone else. In Christianity, we need to be careful of our own words and actions to ensure we do not offend other Christians, even when they have different convictions from us for the non-essentials of faith.
See also "Brotherly Kindness".

Patient Endurance — 11, 36-39, 41, 43
The fifth of eight disciplines outlined in 2 Peter 1:5-7. It is visible by others through our response as we endure suffering. We need Christ to be the "juice" that comes out of us when God allows us to be "squeezed" by adversity. The deeper we go in our faith in Christ, the less likely that suffering will spiritually overwhelm and drown us.
See also "Godliness" and "External Disciplines".

Perseverance — 37
See "Patient Endurance"

Phileo — 45, 49
One of four common Greek words for love. Unlike agape love, it implies a conditional love that is based on respect, admiration and affection. The acts of love that are shown by this love tend to require the love be mutual or returned.
See also "Brotherly Kindness".

Index and Glossary by Subject (continued)

The definitions below are primarily in context of their usage within this Discipleship Guide.

Subject	Page #
Prayer	7, 34

A general discipline in the Christian life of simply communicating with God usually in worship, confession, thanksgiving, and/or supplication.

Subject	Page #
Redemption	22

To re-purchase or buy something back. In Christianity, it refers to the entire salvation process of Jesus sacrificing Himself for us to atone for our sins and in essence paying the price required to "buy" us from the slave market of sin and restore us into right-standing with God.
See also "Salvation".

Subject	Page #
Repentance	16, 19, 24

It's not just simply expressing sorrow or remorse for our sins. In words, it's confessing our sins to God and asking for forgiveness. In actions, it's turning from the very sins we're asking God to forgive in the same way someone driving East on a road would stop and turn around to head West (now heading in the opposite direction).
See also "Sin" and "Faith".

Subject	Page #
Resurrection	11, 20-23, 25, 27, 37, 50, 52, 54

The last of three essential parts of saving faith. Specifically, it's when Jesus was raised on the third day after being crucified and completing the work of atonement for us. Once we're saved and adopted into God's family, He deposits His Holy Spirit in us; this serves as a guarantee and strong hope that the same Holy Spirit Who raised Jesus from the dead will also raise us up to forever live with Him.
See also "Judgment".

Subject	Page #
Revelation	14, 30, 38

The method of revealing something. In this guide, it refers to the method God uses to reveal Himself to people. In a general way, He reveals Himself through His creation to all people. In a special way, He reveals Himself through our conscience to all people and through His commandments to His people (Jews first, then Christians). Finally in a personal way He reveals Himself through conviction and His calling to all Christian believers.
See also "Creation" and "Commandments".

Subject	Page #
Righteousness	24, 27

The state or position of being declared "right". In Christianity, we were once indebted to God by our sin, but the atonement reflects God's mercy by erasing that debt. The resurrection reflects God's grace by His allowing the Holy Spirit to be deposited into us so that we can become a new creation in right standing before Him now with Christ living through us.

Subject #	Page #
Sacrifice	18, 24, 48-51

To give something of extreme value; the value is generally determined by the giver.
See also "Love".

Subject #	Page #
Salvation	8-10, 16, 19, 21, 23, 30, 33, 37, 50, 54

The three stage process of being saved or rescued from sin and restored to right-standing with God. The three stages are 1) Justification (when we were saved and free from the penalty of sin); 2) Sanctification (when we are being saved and free from the power of sin); and 3) Glorification (when we will be saved and free from the presence of sin).
See also "Redemption", "Condemnation" and "Faith".

Subject #	Page #
Sanctification	10, 54

The third of four stages in a Christian's life that represents the period of time from the point of justification (spiritual rebirth) to the point glorification (physical death). It is the time period when we are growing in our faith and living to become life Christ. It is in this stage in the present time that we are being saved and are free from the power of sin.
See also "Faith" and "Glorification".

Subject #	Page #
Saved	9-10, 18, 20, 23, 54

The state of having gone through salvation or being justified.
See also "Salvation".

Subject #	Page #
Scripture	5, 14, 30-31, 37, 50-55

The Bible or God's Word in written form. The Bible itself refers to scripture generally in reference to what was considered the written form of God's Word in that day. That is, the New Testament refers to scripture as what we now call the Old Testament.
See also "Context".

Subject #	Page #
Self-Control	11, 25, 32-35, 37, 43

The fourth of eight disciplines outlined in 2 Peter 1:5-7. There are two aspects to self-control: 1) Filtering what comes INTO us - this involves carefully guarding against what external things may influence us. Fasting is a secondary discipline for this. 2) Filtering what goes OUT from us - this involves carefully guarding against what internal things may come out of the treasures of our heart. Giving (money, time, etc.) is a secondary discipline for this.
See also "Fasting", "Giving", "Patient Endurance", and "Internal Disciplines".

Subject #	Page #
Sin	10-14-21, 23-27, 32-35, 38, 42-43, 47, 50, 55

Formally, it means to miss the mark or not meet a certain standard. Practically, it means to engage in thoughts or actions that do not meet God's holy standard.
See also "Repentance".

Index and Glossary by Subject (continued)

The definitions below are primarily in context of their usage within this Discipleship Guide.

Subject	Page #

Suffering — 18, 23, 35-39

Something that is difficult, challenging, uncomfortable or painful to us either physically, spiritually, mentally, emotionally, etc. The Bible states that suffering can not only be expected as part of the normal Christian life, but it should even be considered a privilege. When God allows suffering in our lives, it's generally an opportunity for us to grow in the discipline of patient endurance.
See "Patient Endurance".

Tabloid Theology — 52, 54

A spiritual belief that is based on sensationalized hearsay and not clearly grounded in scripture. It is generally characterized by a belief based on emotions, experiences or modern stories that sound spiritual, but have no or very weak biblical support (e.g., spiritual dreams or prophecies or stories of angelic visitations or over-emphasizing current events with the book of Revelation). There may be nothing inherently wrong with these, but they should not influence our essential beliefs especially if they contradict any part of scripture.
See also "Folk Theology", "Doctrine", and "Non-Essentials of Faith".

Temperance — 33

See "Self-Control".

Tolerance — 46, 54

See "Consideration".

Virtue — 25

See "Moral Excellence".

Works — 13, 23, 31

Actions or behaviors that can be visible. In Christianity, our salvation is not based on works - we can never do anything to restore our broken relationship with God and earn the salvation we desperately need. Although our salvation requires faith alone, that faith is always followed by actions or works that testify to the faith we confess.
See also "Faith".

The salvation process through the life of a Christian can be summarized by the following four steps:

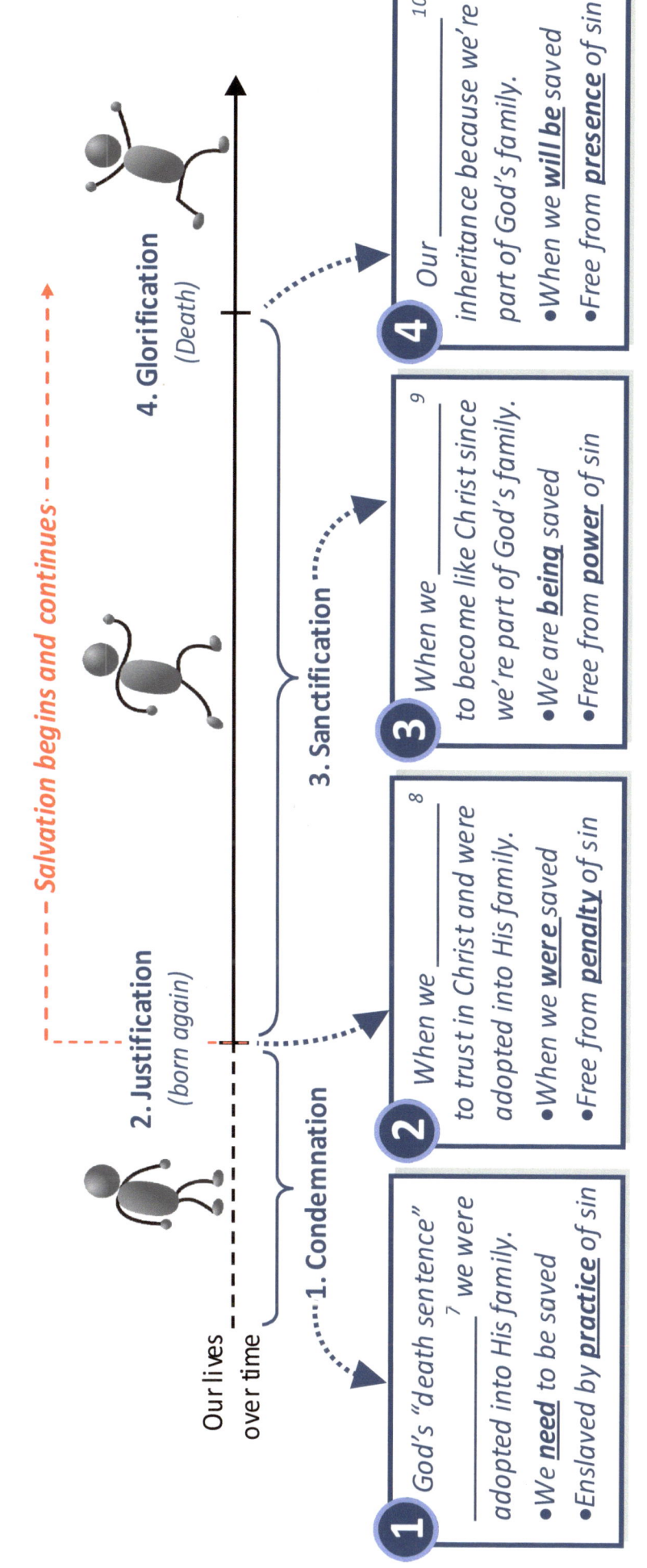

From Lesson 1, page 10

2 Peter 1:5-7 describes 8 disciplines that will help us become like Christ:

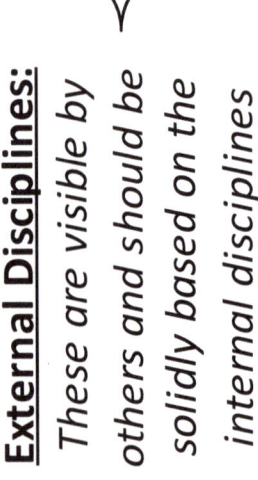

External Disciplines:
These are visible by others and should be solidly based on the internal disciplines

- Love
- Brotherly Kindness
- Godliness
- Patient Endurance

Internal Disciplines:
These are not visible by others and are like layers of underground bedrock upon which the external disciplines are built

- Self Control
- Knowledge
- Moral Excellence
- Faith

From Lesson 1, page 11

The Bible describes our salvation like a legal transaction where God wipes away our debt and makes a "promissory note" (like a promise to pay) for our future redemption. Below is an illustration:

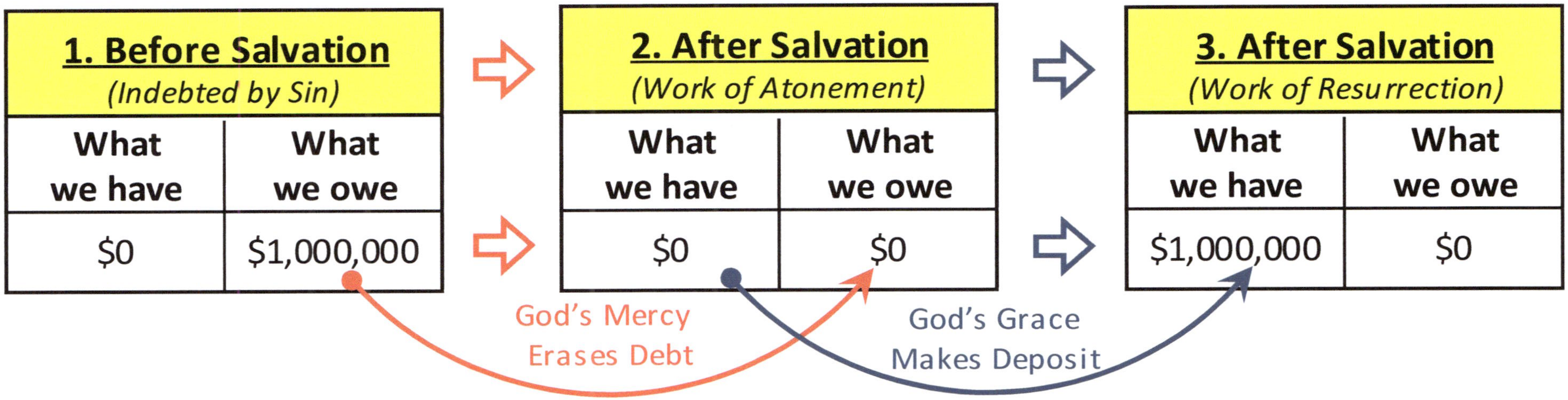

1. Before Salvation (Indebted by Sin)	
What we have	What we owe
$0	$1,000,000

⇨ God's Mercy Erases Debt

2. After Salvation (Work of Atonement)	
What we have	What we owe
$0	$0

⇨ God's Grace Makes Deposit

3. After Salvation (Work of Resurrection)	
What we have	What we owe
$1,000,000	$0

From Lesson 4, page 23

Self control is like a gatekeeper to our heart and mind to perform two basic functions:

1. **Filters what comes INTO us**
(the external influences we absorb internally)

2. **Filters what goes OUT from us**
(the treasures of our heart we express externally)

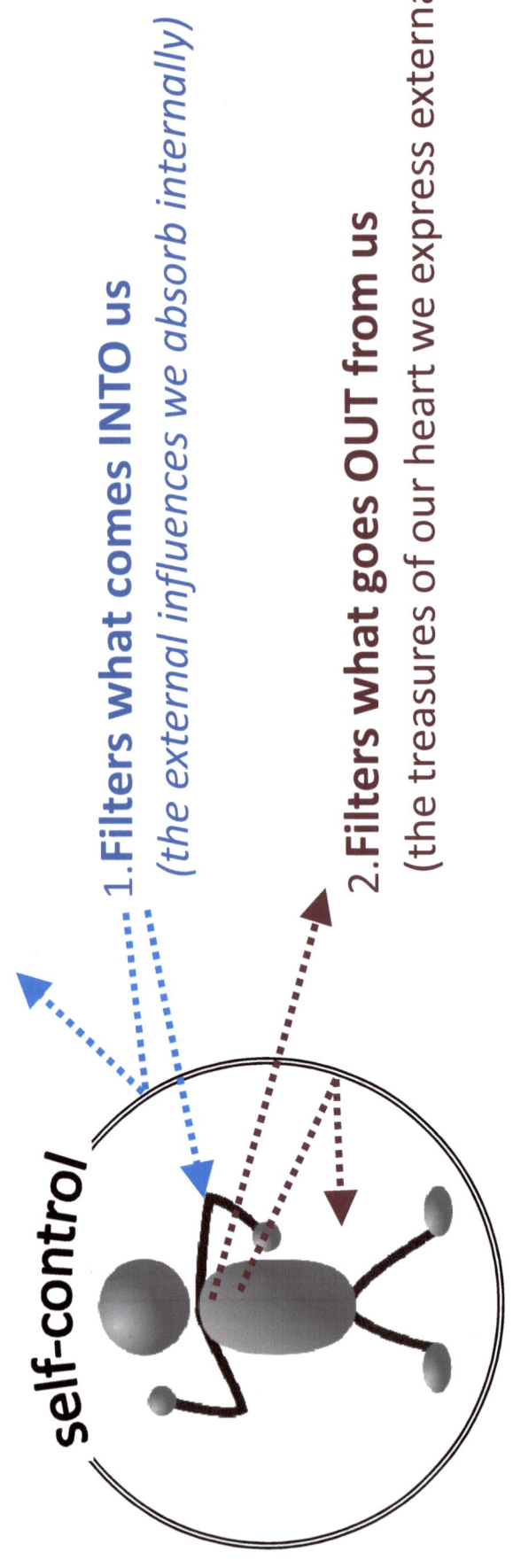

self-control

From Lesson 7, page 33

A tsunami is a huge tidal wave generally caused by an earthquake in the middle of the ocean. Just like throwing a rock in a pool of water, the rippling waves from the energy of the earthquake extend outward until they reach land. When the water is deep, the waves may only be a few feet high and hardly noticeable by anyone out at sea. As the wave approaches shore where the water is more shallow, it forces the water upward to create a massive, destructive wave.

In the same way, the deeper Christians go in their faith in Christ is like going into deeper waters, while those who are shallow in their faith may be like those in shallow water near the shoreline. When adversity comes (like an earthquake), those in deeper waters are unaffected. But those near the shoreline are most vulnerable to the destructive impact from the rising waves of adversity.

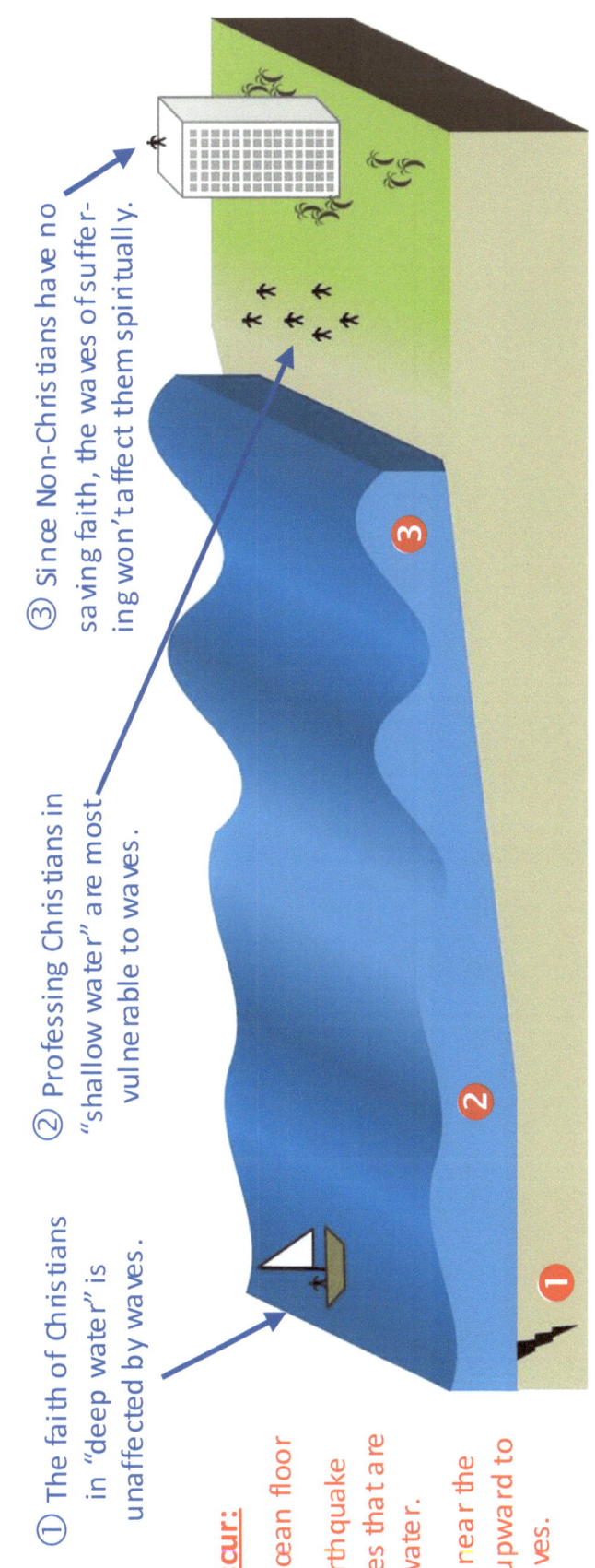

① The faith of Christians in "deep water" is unaffected by waves.

② Professing Christians in "shallow water" are most vulnerable to waves.

③ Since Non-Christians have no saving faith, the waves of suffering won't affect them spiritually.

How Tsunamis Occur:

❶ Earthquake in ocean floor

❷ Energy from earthquake causes rippling waves that are very small in deep water.

❸ Shallow ground near the shore forces water upward to make enormous waves.

From Lesson 8, page 38

70

As the timeline below illustrates, before the time of Christ God's people grew in their knowledge about their faith through stories, then through the Law, and eventually through the additional writings that make up the Old Testament. In the first century, God revealed Himself to His people through Jesus which they expressed through their own writings which make up the New Testament. Even though this is how God has created His inspired Word (our Bible) over time, it is still only a tool that points us to His most inspired and living Word: Christ.

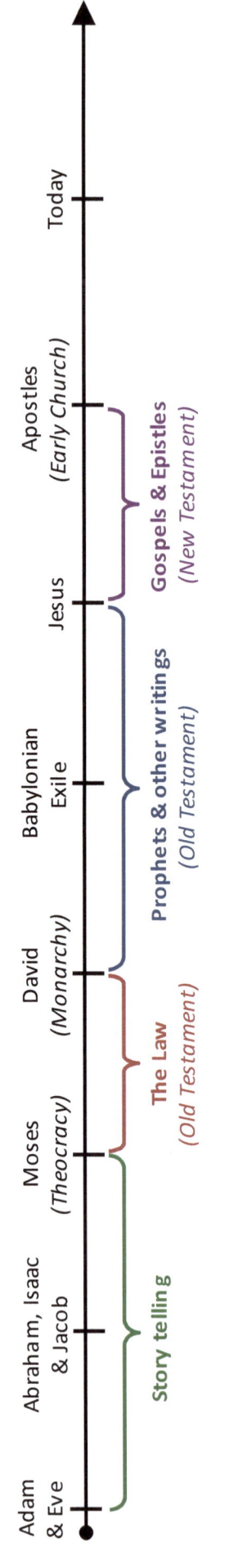

From Lesson 6, page 30

Church doctrine has significantly evolved over the last few thousand years. Over time we have come to a better and more accurate understanding of scripture and formalized that understanding into various doctrines, such as the trinity, the rapture, the infallibility of scripture, and even the atonement.

If salvation is "historically timeless", then what a person in 200 A.D. believed in order to be saved did not necessarily include the doctrines defined after 200 A.D. In other words, a person could've been saved in 200 A.D. and possibly had beliefs that contradicted today's church doctrines.

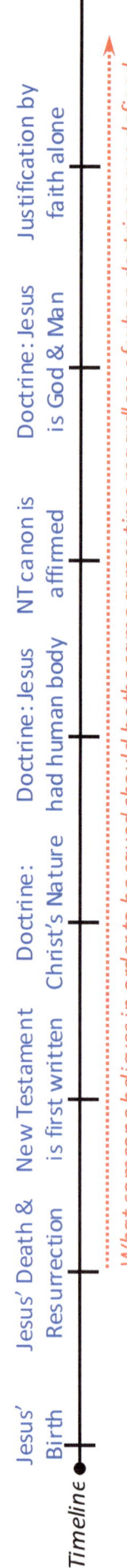

From Lesson 12, page 54

How do we interpret the Bible in the right context?

Don't just ask "what does that scripture mean to *me*?". But instead we should ask "What does that scripture mean?" We should understand the original intent of the scripture to see how God intends for us to apply it to our lives. Here is a three step method for interpreting a scripture in the right context:

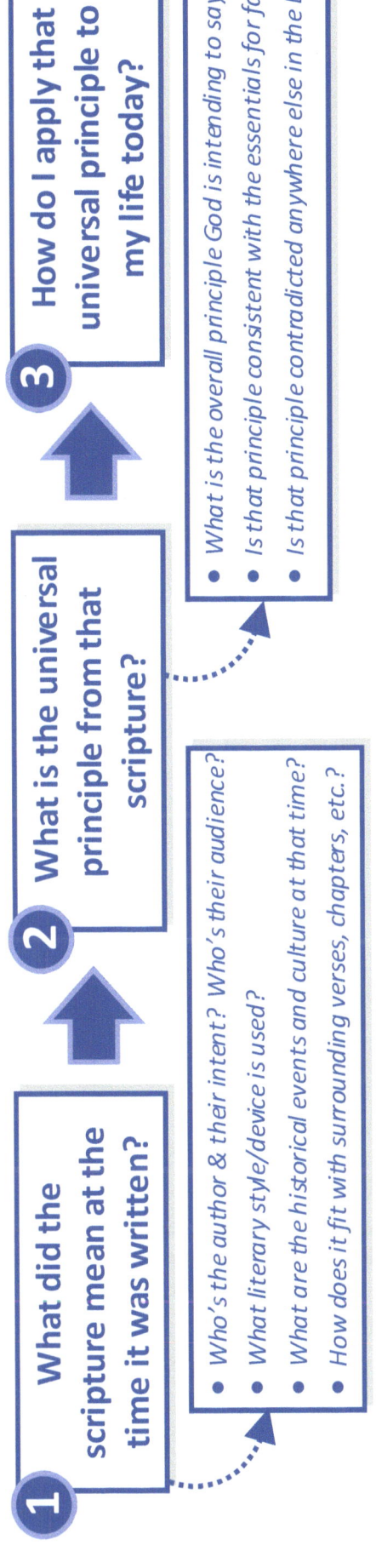

From Lesson 12, page 55

www.ingramcontent.com/pod-product-compliance
Lightning Source LLC
Chambersburg PA
CBHW060755090426
42736CB00002B/44